South East
MountainBiking
North & South Downs

VERTEBRATE PUBLISHING

Design and production by Vertebrate Publishing, Sheffield
www.v-publishing.co.uk

South East
MountainBiking
North & South Downs

Written by
Nick Cotton

Photography by **Andy Heading**

South East
MountainBiking
North & South Downs

VG Copyright © 2008 Vertebrate Graphics Ltd & Nick Cotton

VP Published by Vertebrate Publishing

All rights reserved. No part of this work covered by the copyright hereon may be reproduced
or used in any form or by any means – graphic, electronic,
or mechanised, including photocopying, recording, taping, or information
storage and retrieval systems – without the written permission of the publisher.

ISBN: 978-1-906148-03-4

Cover photo: Susie Farnsworth on the Puttenham Common route.
All Photography by **Andy Heading** unless stated.

Design & production by Nathan Ryder. Maps produced by Nathan Ryder,
Simon Norris and Oliver Jackson – Vertebrate Publishing
www.**v-publishing**.co.uk

Every effort has been made to achieve accuracy of information in this guidebook.
The authors, publishers and copyright owners can take no responsibility for: loss or injury
(including fatal) to persons; loss or damage to property or equipment; trespass,
irresponsible riding or any other mishap that may be suffered as a result of following
the route descriptions or advice offered in this guidebook. The inclusion of a track or path
as part of a route, or otherwise recommended, in this guidebook does not guarantee that
the track or path will remain a Right of Way. If conflict with landowners arises we advise
that you act politely and leave by the shortest route available. If the matter needs to be
taken further then please take it up with the relevant authority.

PLEASE GIVE WAY TO HORSES AND PEDESTRIANS.

Contents

SECTION 1 – THE NORTH DOWNS

ROUTE GRADES
▲ = EASY ▲ = MODERATE ▲ = HARD (see page x)

SECTION 2 – THE SOUTH DOWNS

KEY TO THE MAP SYMBOLS

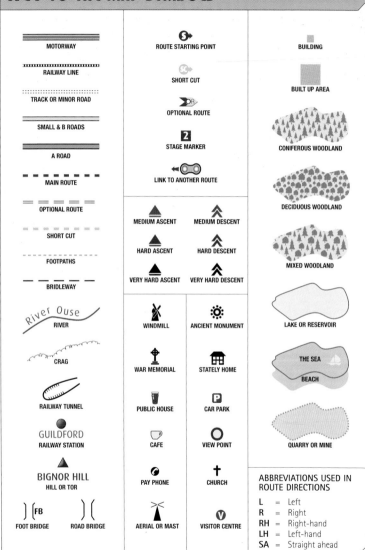

MOTORWAY

RAILWAY LINE

TRACK OR MINOR ROAD

SMALL & B ROADS

A ROAD

MAIN ROUTE

OPTIONAL ROUTE

SHORT CUT

FOOTPATHS

BRIDLEWAY

River Ouse
RIVER

CRAG

RAILWAY TUNNEL

GUILDFORD
RAILWAY STATION

BIGNOR HILL
HILL OR TOR

FB
FOOT BRIDGE   ROAD BRIDGE

ROUTE STARTING POINT

SHORT CUT

OPTIONAL ROUTE

2
STAGE MARKER

LINK TO ANOTHER ROUTE

MEDIUM ASCENT   MEDIUM DESCENT

HARD ASCENT   HARD DESCENT

VERY HARD ASCENT   VERY HARD DESCENT

WINDMILL   ANCIENT MONUMENT

WAR MEMORIAL   STATELY HOME

PUBLIC HOUSE   CAR PARK

CAFE   VIEW POINT

PAY PHONE   CHURCH

AERIAL OR MAST   VISITOR CENTRE

BUILDING

BUILT UP AREA

CONIFEROUS WOODLAND

DECIDUOUS WOODLAND

MIXED WOODLAND

LAKE OR RESERVOIR

THE SEA
BEACH

QUARRY OR MINE

ABBREVIATIONS USED IN ROUTE DIRECTIONS

L   = Left
R   = Right
RH = Right-hand
LH = Left-hand
SA = Straight ahead

Introduction

Among the first bike guides I ever wrote was one covering Kent, Surrey and Sussex. It was a surprise then to discover the dense network of byways and bridleways criss-crossing the North and South Downs, offering an entry to a parallel world – one far removed from the teeming millions in their cars on the busy roads and in offices and shopping malls.

That sense of surprise and that concept of a 'parallel world' have not been diminished over the years. Each time I return to the South Downs, I am convinced that the 100-mile long South Downs Way, from Winchester to Eastbourne, can hold its head high as one of the finest long-distance mountain bike routes in Britain. It is a great rollercoaster along the whaleback chalk ridge, with views out over the English Channel on one side and down to the Sussex Weald on the other, and has challenging climbs and fast descents to satisfy the fittest riders.

This book offers a selection of 24 rides and gives a taste of the variety of riding that can be found south of London, from the tough sandy climbs up through pine woods to Leith Hill, the highest point in South East England at a mighty 294m/965ft, to the string of beacons along the chalk ridge that forms the South Downs, from Butser Hill in the west, past Chanctonbury Ring, Ditchling and Firle Beacons, and as far as Willingdon Hill overlooking the sea at Eastbourne.

These are not remote moorland rides over misty peat tracks. You are never more than a few miles from the nearest town with bike shops, cafés and pubs, so breakdowns, hunger and thirst can all easily be dealt with. There is, however, a different sort of warning for rides in the area: WINTER MUD. You may be the fittest rider around and your bike may weigh less than 10 kilos, but in the depths of winter, or after several days of prolonged rain, many of these trails will coat you and your bike in inches of gloop. It's hard to find good snow for skiing in summer and it's hard to find good mountain biking on chalk in winter.

So go out and enjoy, let us know what you think of the routes, ride them clockwise and anticlockwise, link them together and personalise them. They should get better and better as you ride them more often, so you have your eyes on the trail, not on the map.

Nick Cotton

Acknowledgements

Our thanks to a few people:

Susie Farnsworth, Tom Fenton, Jared Pace and James Freeborough for being great models for the photo shoots and Andy Heading for his excellent work in taking the photographs. At Vertebrate Publishing, Nathan Ryder for his design and production work, Jon Barton and Simon Norris for their backing and earlier work and Oliver Jackson for his proof reading.

How to Use This Book

Riding in the North & South Downs

The North and South Downs are two ridges of hills that lie to the south of London, rising in both cases to almost 300m/1000ft and offering the best mountain biking in Surrey, Sussex and Kent. In such a densely populated area, the network of tracks offers an escape into a parallel world of woodland and pasture, stitching together sections of bridleways and byways that bypass the towns and busy roads, leading you away from the crowds. The tracks tend to be well-signposted and generally well-maintained and, this being the South East, there's no chance of being stranded by the weather on some bleak boggy moorland track, miles from anywhere.

Both the North and South Downs have a National Trail running along their entire length. There are some similarities but there are several differences:

The North Downs Way, which stretches from Farnham to Canterbury, passes through more built-up areas, offers a mixture of chalk tracks and sandy tracks, and most importantly, can only be ridden in parts: long sections have only footpath status. Ride on the footpaths and you will get an earful from the regular walkers, and not make it any easier for the rest of us who tend to get tarred with the same brush.

The South Downs Way runs from Winchester to Eastbourne, over a series of highpoints or beacons, with big views out to the English Channel and down into the Weald. It is one long chalk ridge, cut through by the occasional river and has bridleway or byway status along its entire length so thumbs up for mountain biking.

A word about mud... (read this if nothing else)

Mountain biking in South East England in the winter months, or after prolonged rain, can at times be all but impossible. The chalk and clay turns to a claggy mass which sticks to your wheels and chain, doubling the weight of the bike while halving your options for gears. This is real Jekyll and Hyde stuff, as the same tracks in summer offer fast excellent biking and it's hard to see how they could change so dramatically from one season to the next.

The rides have all been researched from late spring to mid autumn and, where possible, I have tried to guess where the mud will be worst and suggested road alternatives. From late autumn to late spring it is definitely a case of tailoring your rides to suit conditions. Find the location of your nearest garage with a jet wash.

A word about sand... (OK, you should read this as well)

The tracks through the North Downs use a mixture of chalk tracks (as per the South Downs) but also sandy tracks, as there is a geological stratum running parallel with the chalk ridge all the way from Alton to Folkestone. Hard packed sand is a delight – fast draining and rideable all year round. Soft sand is very hard work, at times you have to push your bike DOWNHILL! I've tried to minimise time on tracks such as this. Sandy tracks will be your best bet in the winter months.

A word about horses... (another important bit!)

There are many horse riders in the South East of England and a surprising number of horses seem to be unsure about mountain bikes. In order to avoid injury to yourself, your bike, the horse and the rider (rearrange the order of priority as you see fit), SLOW DOWN and make yourself heard. If you are about to zoom down a hill and see horses coming up towards you, take a breather, wait till they have passed then enjoy the descent. If you come up behind horses, say "hello" and let the horse hear a voice so that it knows you are a human. Be prepared to stop and pull in to one side for particularly skittish horses. Horseriders are almost always grateful for any courtesy shown and a few seconds added to your ride time is hardly the end of the world.

The Routes

There are 10 rides in the North Downs and 14 in the South Downs, more or less reflecting the density of bridleways in the respective areas. The guide doesn't claim to be definitive but will give you a good taste of the whole area. Try the rides as described, in reverse, link them together, tweak them for different weather conditions.

Each route will improve as you ride it a second and third time and you can concentrate on the trails and not have your nose buried in the maps and route instructions.

Grades

Routes, climbs and descents are graded blue, red and black, in a similar system to that used at several of the trail centres around the UK.

▲ = Easy   ▲ = Moderate   ▲ = Hard

Most of the routes are graded red with an average total height gain of 300m–500m. There is very little (legal) technical singletrack, so a black route is given that grade for the greater number of climbs, not for its technical challenges. Of course, following on from what has been said about winter riding, the easiest trail could become a black grade marathon if you are faced with endless mud.

Route Descriptions & Accuracy

All the routes have been ridden at least twice to ensure accuracy but things change – signs disappear, new signs are put up, vegetation is cut back or left to grow unchecked, a field is ploughed, tracks are occasionally improved, or more often damaged by horses/scramble bikes/4x4s when the surface is soft. If a route instruction appears at odds with what you can see, check the appropriate Ordnance Survey map.

Woodland route directions

These can be a nightmare for author and riders. Where there are no signs or obvious landmarks, it is important when making your way through wooded areas to weigh up each word of description: 'broad' or 'narrow' track, 'gently' uphill or 'steeply' uphill, 'bear' left or 'turn sharply' left, 'earth' track or 'stone' track and so on. A compass can sometimes be useful to ensure you are not heading in completely the wrong direction.

While on the subject of woodlands, for all you twisty rooty singletrack aficionados, you'll have to make up your own routes as, with the exception of the 'Summer Lightning' Forestry Commission route on Leith Hill near Dorking, there are no purpose-built routes of the type you will find in the forest centres in Wales and Scotland. There are some easier, waymarked trails in Queen Elizabeth Country Park south of Petersfield and in Friston Forest west of Eastbourne.

Rights of Way

Countryside access in the UK hasn't been particularly kind to cyclists, although things are improving. We have 'right of way' on bridleways (blue arrows on signs) and byways (red arrows). However, having 'right of way' doesn't actually mean having the right of way, just that we're allowed to ride there – so give way to walkers and horse riders. We're also allowed to ride on green lanes and some unclassified roads, although the only way to determine which are legal and which aren't is to check with the local countryside authority. Obviously, cycle routes are also in.

The very understanding Forestry Commission generally allows cyclists to use its land (again, you'll need to check with them first to be sure). You must, however, obey all signs, especially those warning of forestry operations – a fully loaded logging truck will do more than scuff your frame...

Everything else is out of bounds (unless the landowner says otherwise). Riding illegally can upset walkers, (who have every right to enjoy their day); is, in many cases, technically classed as trespass (meaning you could be prosecuted for any damage caused) and can damage fragile moorland. **Please don't do it**.

Not all tracks are signed, so it's not always obvious whether that great-looking trail you want to follow is an illegal footpath or a legal bridleway. That's why it's a good idea to carry a map with you on every ride.

The Bike

Any half-decent mountain bike will be fine (try and avoid a "£99 special"). A full suspension bike will add comfort and control. A lightweight race number will make hills easier and something with a bit of travel will help on technical descents. We'd pick a compromise somewhere between the three, depending on your personal preferences.

Check everything's working – you won't be going uphill fast if your gears seize but equally you'll be a little quicker than planned if your brakes fail coming down. Pump the tyres up, check nothing's about to wear through and make sure that everything that should be tight is tight.

Essential Kit

Helmet
"The best helmet is the one that you're wearing". Make sure it fits, you're wearing it correctly and that it won't move in a crash.

Clothing
You need to get your clothing right if you want to stay comfortable on a bike, especially in bad weather. The easiest way to do this is to follow a layering system. Begin with clothing made from 'technical' synthetic or wool fabrics that will wick the sweat away from your body and then dry quickly, keeping you dry and warm. Stay away from cotton – it absorbs moisture and holds onto it. If it's chilly, an insulating layer will keep you warm, and a wind/waterproof layer on the outside protects from the elements. Layers can then be removed or added to suit the conditions. Padded shorts are more comfortable, but the amount of lycra on display is down to you. Baggy shorts, full length tights and trousers are all available to match the conditions.

Set off a little on the cold side – you'll soon warm up. Don't leave the warm clothes behind though, as the weather can turn quickly.

Gloves
Gloves ward off blisters and numb hands and help keep your fingers warm. They also provide a surprising amount of protection when you come off.

Footwear
Flat pedals/clips-ins – it's your call. Make sure you can walk in them and that they have sufficient tread for you to do so. Consider overshoes if it's chilly.

Other Essentials
As mentioned, take any necessary spares, tools, tube and pump, spare clothes, first aid kit, food and water. Stop short of the kitchen sink, as you'll still want to be able to actually ride your bike.

You'll need something to carry this lot in. We'd suggest a hydration pack, as they allow you to drink on the move and keep excess weight off the bike.

Ordnance Survey Landranger Maps

For the North Downs rides:

For the South Downs rides:

Night Riding

Night riding is ace! It's possible to enjoy an after-work ride in the depths of winter in your favourite off-road playground. But it's a completely different ball game and (hardly surprisingly) there are a few risks to be aware of.

Lights and Batteries

Invest carefully in a lighting system. Consider battery life, weight, number/type of bulbs and power. Fully charge your battery before a ride (sounds like common sense, until you forget). Carry a secondary light source (such as a head torch) for emergencies (it's surprising what you can ride with a commuter light if you have to, although it isn't much fun). Pack a rear light for road sections and keep it clean.

Route Planning and Safety

Choose your ride on the basis of battery life. Time it yourself, don't necessarily rely on the manufacturer's information. Allow extra time – you'll be slower in the dark. Stay on ground that you are familiar with at first (night-time navigation in unfamiliar territory demands military expertise) and not too far from home. Ride with a friend. Watch out for the were-wolves. Tell someone you're out.

Ride within your limits – trees loom up very quickly in the dark!

General Safety

The ability to read a map, navigate in poor visibility and to understand weather warnings is essential. Don't head out in bad weather, unless you're confident and capable of doing so.

Some of the routes described point you at tough climbs and steep descents that can potentially be very dangerous. Too much exuberance on a steep descent in the middle of nowhere and you could be in more than a spot of bother, especially if you're alone. Consider your limitations and relative fragility.

Be self-sufficient. Carry food and water, spares, a tube and a pump. Consider a first-aid kit. Even if it's warm, the weather could turn, so take a wind/waterproof. Think about what could happen on an enforced stop. Pack lights if you could finish in the dark.

If you're riding solo, think about the seriousness of an accident – you might be without help for a very long time. Tell someone where you're going, when you'll be back and tell them once you are back. Take a mobile phone if you have one, but don't expect a signal. And **don't** call out the ambulance because you've grazed your knee.

Riding in a group is safer (ambitious overtaking manoeuvers excepted) and often more fun, but don't leave slower riders too far behind and give them a minute for a breather when they've caught up. Allow extra time for a group ride, as you'll inevitably stop and chat. You might need an extra top if you're standing around for a while. Ride within your ability, make sure you can slow down fast and give way to other users. Bells might be annoying, but they work. If you can't bring yourself to bolt one on, a polite 'excuse me' should be fine.

On hot, sunny days, slap on some Factor 30+ and ALWAYS WEAR YOUR HELMET!

In the Event of an Accident

In the event of an accident requiring immediate assistance: Dial 999 and ask for **POLICE** or **AMBULANCE**. If you can supply the services with a grid reference of exactly where you are it should help to speed up their response time.

Rules of the (Off) Road

1. Always ride on legal trails.
2. Ride considerately – give way to horses and pedestrians.
3. Don't spook animals.
4. Ride in control – you don't know who's around the next corner.
5. Leave gates as you find them – if you're unsure, shut them.
6. Keep the noise down and don't swear loudly when you fall off in front of walkers.
7. Leave no trace – take home everything you took out.
8. Keep water sources clean – don't take toilet stops near streams.
9. Enjoy the countryside and respect its life and work.

Planning Your Ride

1. Consider the ability/experience of each rider in your group. Check the weather forecast. How much time do you have available? Now choose your route.
2. Study the route description before setting off, and cross-reference it with the relevant map.
3. Bear in mind everything we've suggested about safety, clothing, spares and food and drink.
4. Get out there and get dirty.

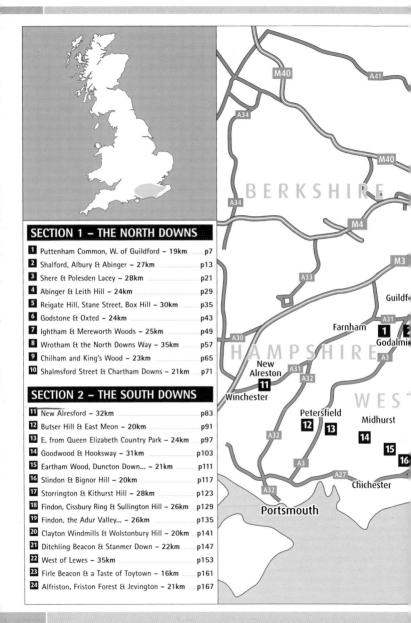

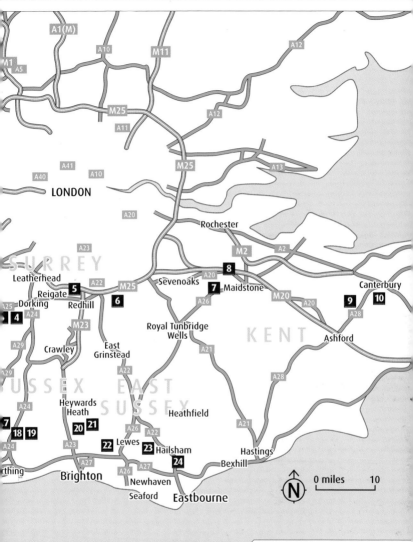

SECTION 1

North Downs

Thread your way through secret passageways of sand, chalk and flint beneath canopies of trees. Emerge blinking at a main road and dive back into the network of trails that magically link together, offering you a radically different view of Surrey and Kent.

North Downs
sponsored by

www.lumicycle.com

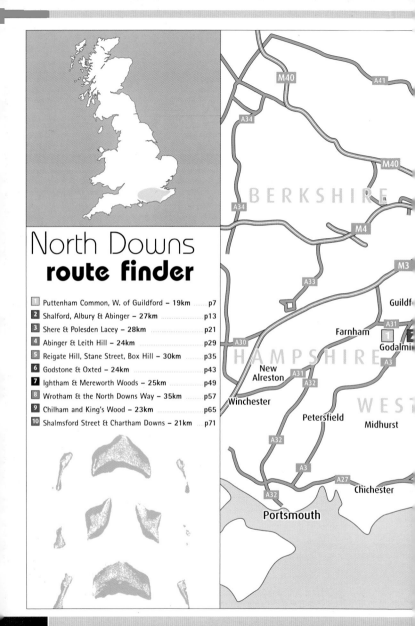

North Downs
route finder

BERKSHIRE

HAMPSHIRE

WEST

M40

A41

A34

M40

M4

M3

A33

Guildf

A31

Farnham

Godalmi

A30

A3

New
Alreston

A31

A32

Winchester

Petersfield

Midhurst

A32

A3

A27

Chichester

A32

Portsmouth

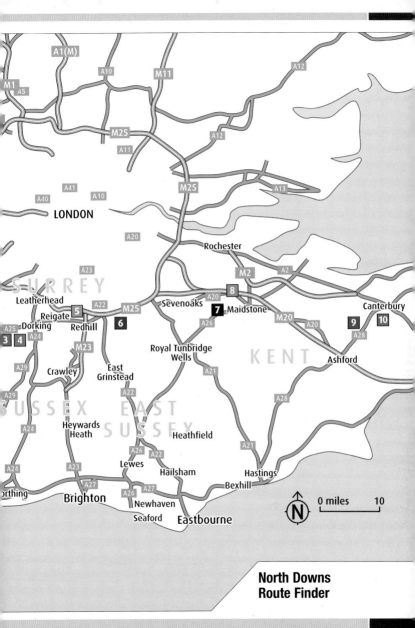

**North Downs
Route Finder**

1 Puttenham Common, West of Guildford

Introduction

The North Downs Way starts in Farnham, but the first few miles have footpath status, so it's no go for mountain biking. The mixed status of footpath/bridleway/byway for the North Downs Way continues all the way to Dover. This is in contrast to the South Downs Way, which is open to mountain bikers along its whole length. This ride explores the sandy tracks to the west of Guildford, starting with a bridleway playground on Puttenham Common, which you may find it difficult to tear yourself away from as there are bucketfuls of top grade tracks.

The Ride

Enjoy the fine tracks heading north over Puttenham Common before picking up the North Downs Way as it heads east. Beyond Puttenham, you enter one of those parallel worlds where you find yourself on good tracks through beautiful woodland – then you look at the map and realise you were never far from dual carriageways full of men in suits and supermarket trucks. Turn south and weave your way through Hurtmore on ever so narrow tracks (leggings recommended) to cross the A3 again and re-enter that wonderful maze of 'hidden' bridleways back to the car park.

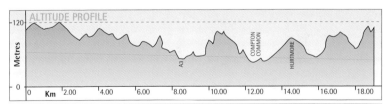

ALTITUDE PROFILE

Metres: 120 — 0

Km: 0 | 2.00 | 4.00 | 6.00 | 8.00 | 10.00 | 12.00 | 14.00 | 16.00 | 18.00

(labels on profile: A3, COMPTON COMMON, HURTMORE)

PUTTENHAM COMMON, WEST OF GUILDFORD   GRADE: ▲

DISTANCE: 19KM

START/FINISH: PUTTENHAM COMMON CAR PARK

PARKING: AS ABOVE AT GR 920 462

TOTAL ASCENT: 150M

GRID REFERENCE: GR 920 462

CAFÉ: BRING SANDWICHES

PUBLIC HOUSE: GOOD INTENT, PUTTENHAM Tel: 01483 810 387. WITHIES INN, COMPTON Tel: 01483 421 158. THE STAG, EASHING Tel: 01483 421 568.

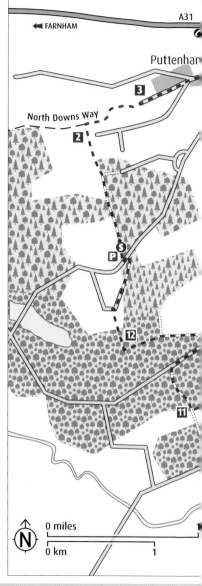

**Puttenham Common,
West of Guildford**

Directions – Puttenham Common, West of Guildford

➎ Go along the **RH** edge of the Puttenham Common car park to exit at the far **RH** corner, following a line of low wooden posts. Follow this excellent sand and earth track in the same direction, **ignoring** turns to the right and left (there are too many tracks in the woods to mention each junction).

2 After 1.5km, at a T-junction with a wire fence in a bank of ferns ahead, turn **R** gently uphill, soon descending on sand. After 500m, at the next T-junction, turn **L** towards a wooden post with a purple arrow. Shortly, at a third T-junction, with a red-brick house 100m to the left and a telegraph pole ahead, turn **R** uphill (red arrow).

3 Climb, descend then climb again, following red arrows and *North Downs Way* (acorn) signs on the main sand and stone track. Join tarmac by a house called Clouds Hill to the left.

4 At the T-junction with The Street at the end of Lascombe Lane, bear **R** through Puttenham. Go past the Good Intent pub and a church. At the T-junction with the busy B3000, turn **R** towards Compton. Shortly, turn **L** opposite the Jolly Farmers (Harvester) pub, onto a wide gravel track, signposted *North Downs Way*.

5 Keep following *North Downs Way/National Cycle Network Route 22* signs in the same direction at several track junctions. Some of these may be obscured by vegetation. Join tarmac and bear **R**, passing under two road bridges. At a T-junction with a road (GR 958 477) turn **L** towards Guildford, then **R** onto a broad, sandy track, signposted *North Downs Way*. (May be soft.)

6 Beyond the barns is a push on a narrower, soft sand track. Shortly, at a X-roads of bridleways, with several *Loseley Estate* signs in the trees, leave the North Downs Way and turn **R** downhill. At tarmac continue downhill. After 600m take the first road **L** by a triangle of grass, passing Withies pub.

7 At the offset X-roads with busy New Pond Road (B3000), turn **R** then **L** onto The Avenue. **Easy to miss**: after 100m, turn **R** onto a rough earth track, signposted *Bridleway*. Continue **SA** at X-roads with a footpath, following the bridleway along the hedge and up through the field, climbing towards the woodland ahead.

8   At the wood turn **R** and follow this track, with trees to your left. At the end of a fenced field, jink **R** then **L**, following blue arrows and climbing steeply. Continue in the same direction on a broad gravel drive, going **SA** at X-roads with two roads, following *Bridleway* signs. These sections may be overgrown.

9   At the T-junction with a broader earth track at the bottom of the descent, turn **L** to continue downhill. At the offset X-roads with a wall and house to the right, turn **R** then **L**. Go through a field gate and continue in the same direction on a concrete track. At the road, turn **R*** ▶OR▶ then **R** again by the petrol station, up across the bridge over the A3.

    * ▶OR▶ turn **L** for the Stag Inn, Eashing

10   Go through a field gate and turn **R**, following blue arrows around the edge of the field. At the end of the second side of the field, turn **R** through a gate and ride along the edge of the woodland, signposted *Bridleway*. Go **SA** at two X-roads with tarmac, following *Bridleway* signs. Descend and follow the main track round to the **L** along the wooded valley floor.

11   At the X-roads of broad gravel paths, by a yellowy-brown brick house (GR 928 448), turn **R**. At the T-junction with the road, turn **R**. Climb. **Easy to miss**: shortly after the brow and on the descent, turn sharp **L** uphill, back on yourself, on a wide earth and stone track, signposted *Byway*.

12   Climb steadily. At a X-roads of tracks, shortly after the brow of the hill, by a post with red and blue arrows, go **SA** downhill, following the blue arrow. After 200m, turn **R** by the next wooden post with all blue arrows. At the fork, bear **R** onto tarmac and keep bearing **R**. Tarmac turns to track and climbs. Keep following the blue arrows. At the road, turn **L** then **R**, to return to Puttenham Common car park.

◄⊙⊙ Making a day of it

Puttenham Common is criss-crossed with bridleways and could be a playground for many hours – definitely one to explore over and over again. It is easy enough to head due east and link, via lanes and a footbridge over the Wey Navigation at **GR 995 482**, to the start of the **Shalford & Abinger Ride** *(see page 13)*. There are loads of bridleways across Ockley Common and Hankley Common to the southwest of Puttenham although many of these are soft and sandy.

2 Shalford, Albury & Abinger

27km

Introduction

This ride highlights the two contrasting surfaces – sand and clay – that occur through much of the North Downs. Sand, when hard, is fantastic: quick draining and rideable all year round; when soft it is a nightmare where you have to push your bike, even on some downhills. Clay, when smooth and hard, is very fast, but when soft is sticky beyond belief and, if horses or 4x4s have been through, can become bucking bronco territory. Geology lesson over. If you do this ride frequently, you may tailor it to suit the conditions underfoot.

The Ride

One minute you are in Guildford's suburbs and the next you have escaped into a secret world of woodland tracks, totally removed from the noise and pressure of the 21st Century. Push your bike up to St Martha's and slither down the other side. Sand – don't you just love it? Errrm... Weave your way on sandy tracks through woodland glades, bypassing Shere and Gomshall, to climb steeply north beyond the railway crossing, leaving behind sand to enter a world of chalk, clay and flint. Apologies to all those hungry for woodland singletrack – there are loads of narrow tracks in the North Downs woodland and it is impossible to describe them. Treat the main forest roads described in these rides as the framework and make up your own singletrack loops. A gentle woodland descent leads to a fine café at Newlands Corner and you're almost home and dry.

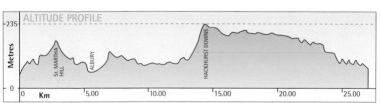

ALTITUDE PROFILE

235

Metres

St. MARTHA'S HILL

ALBURY

HACKHURST DOWNS

0

0   Km   5.00   10.00   15.00   20.00   25.00

SHALFORD, ALBURY & ABINGER   GRADE: ▲

DISTANCE: 27KM
TOTAL ASCENT: 400M
START/FINISH: CAR PARK OFF PILGRIMS WAY/ECHO PIT ROAD OFF THE A281 BETWEEN GUILDFORD AND SHALFORD
GRID REFERENCE: GR 003 484
PARKING: AS OPPOSITE AT GR 003 484
CAFÉ: ABINGER TEASHOP, ABINGER Tel: 01306 730 811
PUBLIC HOUSE: COMPASSES, GOMSHALL Tel: 01483 202 506.
ABINGER ARMS, ABINGER Tel: 01306 730 145

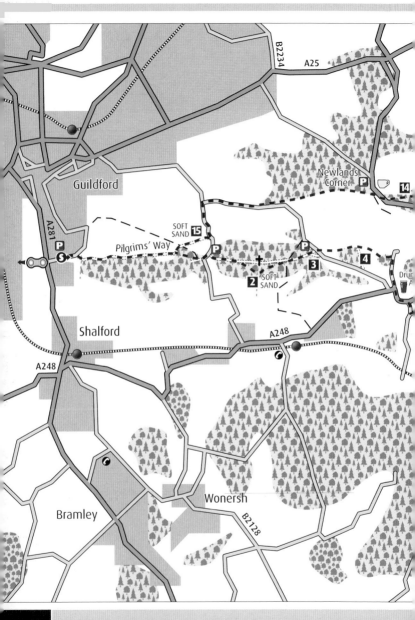

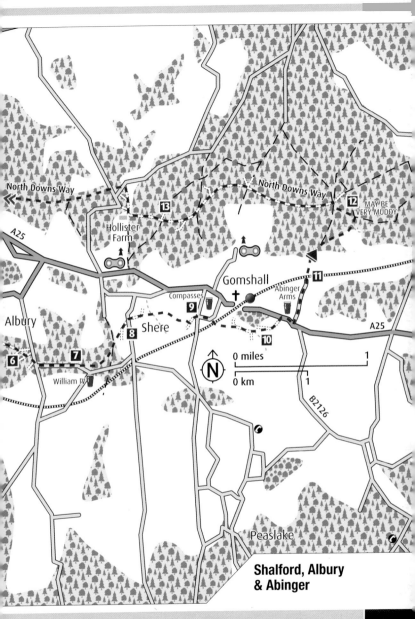

Shalford, Albury & Abinger

Directions – Shalford, Albury & Abinger

❻ Turn **L** out of the Pilgrims Way/Echo Pit Road car park and continue **SA** at a X-roads of tracks, passing to the left of Chantry Cottage. Climb on this fine track through woodland, following signs for *North Downs Way* (acorn) and **ignoring** turnings to the right and left. One soft sand section. After almost 2km, at the T-junction with a lane, turn **L** then **R** steeply uphill, following *North Downs Way* signs.

2 Go past a car park on the left. After 500m, you come to a fork of tracks on the climb, by a 2-way signpost just before a green electricity generator. Bear **R** here, signposted *Bridleway* – the footpath to the left leads to the church. Soft sandy push. At the X-roads of tracks just after the top, with St Martha's church up to the left and fine views to the right, continue **SA** on the bridleway.

3 After 450m, at a fork on the descent, bear **R** towards a wooden *Downs Link* signboard, leaving the North Downs Way. Continue downhill from the small, sandy car park, to the road and turn **R**, then shortly **L** by a 30mph sign, leading onto a narrow sandy track, signposted *Bridleway*.

4 At the X-roads of tracks beneath telephone lines, continue **SA**, signposted *Bridleway*, onto a broad track across a field. Climb, then soon re-enter woodland on a narrower track. At the bottom of a short, steep descent, at the T-junction with a lane, turn **R** downhill.

5 At the T-junction with the A248, at the end of Water Lane, turn **L** then after 300m turn **R** onto Church Lane, opposite the PO/stores in Albury, by an ornate wooden sign. Follow the road past the church. Tarmac turns to track, then swings **R** uphill, with steep embankments on both sides.

6 Steady climb through atmospheric cutting. How much can you ride? At the T-junction with a wider track at the top, bear **L** to continue climbing. After 250m, at a fork of tracks in a wide sandy clearing, bear **R** (blue arrow). Shortly bear **L** to cross a wider gravel track, **SA** uphill onto a similar sandy track (blue arrow).

7 Emerge at the road junction and take Park Road, following signs for *Peaslake*. Go past Heath Lane to the right, then on a **RH** bend, with a modern red-brick house to the left, bear **L** onto a track signposted *Bridleway*. Keep bearing **L** alongside a ramshackle fence to the left. At an obvious fork by a wooden post with two blue arrows, bear **R** on the upper track.

8 At a X-roads on the edge of Shere at the end of Pathfields, go **SA*** ▶OR▷ onto The Spinning Walk. Continue in the same direction as it turns to track. At the T-junction with a gravel drive (Gravelpits Farmhouse is to your right), turn **L**.

> * ▶OR▷ turn **L** here and join the start of the **Shere & Polesden Lacey** ride *(Page 21)*.

9 At the road at the end of Gravelpits Lane, go **SA**, then bear **L** past a wooden bus shelter. After 200m, on a **LH** bend, turn **R** under the railway bridge onto Tower Hill (no through road), and almost immediately, turn **L** onto a wide track, signposted *Bridleway*, and ride past barns. Shortly, at a fork of tracks, bear **L** on the lower track alongside the fence to the left.

10 At a T-junction, bear **R** on a wide gravel track by Twiga Lodge. Shortly, on a **RH** bend, bear **L** by a wooden signpost (blue arrow) and keep following blue arrows. At a concrete track, continue **SA**. At the T-junction with the busy A25, turn **R**. Take the first road **L** by Abinger Arms pub onto a no through road, just before the ornate clocktower on the building ahead.

11 Tarmac turns to track at the final house. Go over the level crossing and start climbing. **Ignore** a left then a right turn. Continue on the main, climbing track, going **SA** at X-roads with a footpath. (There is a *National Trust Blatchford Down* sign on the left). The track levels out.

12 Shortly, at the next major X-roads, by a 4-way *Bridleway* signpost (GR 104 489) turn **L**. This bit is muddy in winter, damaged by 4x4s and scramble bikes. At the T-junction, with a red arrow and a single *Bridleway* fingerpost, turn **L**, following the red arrow. Soon continue in the same direction through a metal gate and an enormous log barrier, signposted *Bridleway*.

13 Becomes a wide, flat, well-surfaced track. Go **SA** at several X-roads. Keep following *North Downs Way* signs past stables and Hollister Farm as the track swings **R** (north). **Ignore** a left turn, then bear **R** at a fork of broad stone tracks. At the road, turn **R**, then sharp **L**, passing to the **L** of a round concrete pond, signposted *North Downs Way*.

DIRECTIONS CONTINUE ON NEXT PAGE

14 Cross the lane into West Hanger car park, following *North Downs Way* signs. Fine, gentle woodland descent. At the T-junction with the A25, follow the path to the **R**, then cross the busy road opposite the Barn Café. Go through the far end of the car park, following blue arrows and *Bridleway* signs. Gently downhill – muddy in winter. At the road, bear **R** to continue downhill.

15 As the road swings right, turn **L** onto Halfpenny Lane. **Easy to miss**: at the bottom of the hill, turn **R** onto a track signposted *Bridleway*. Very soft sand. **Ignore** a right fork towards Pewley Down. At the X-roads of tracks by wooden barriers with a steep track ahead, turn **R** to rejoin the outward route back to the start.

◄━◯◯◯ **Making a day of it**

To the west you can link to the **Puttenham** ride *(page 7)* near Compton via the footbridge over the Wey Navigation at **GR 995 482** and then use the North Downs Way. To the east, this ride overlaps with the **Shere & Polesden Lacey** ride *(page 21)* between Shere and Gomshall. To link the two, follow this ride from Instructions **1** to **8** then go into Shere to join the **Shere & Polesden Lacey** ride at Instruction **1**.

3 Shere & Polesden Lacey

28km

Introduction

Draw a line 10 miles around Dorking and you have some of the best mountain biking on the North Downs – a varied mix of sand and chalk tracks, easy woodland rides, tough climbs up the escarpment and rattling descents down the other side. As ever, on rides featuring chalk, do not attempt this in the depths of winter, as your bike will turn into a barely recognisable monster with clag-caked wheels, each weighing as much as the whole bike normally does. This ride features one of the book's best climbing challenges, at the start from Shere, and one of the best descents, down towards Polesden Lacey.

The Ride

Once past the 4x4 damage near the start, the climb north from Shere is a fine challenge, taking you up to the forested plateau that stretches most of the way between Dorking and Guildford. Go past the sawmill that specialises in hardwoods, located deep in the woodland and surrounded by the huge trunks of ancient oaks. The descent towards Polesden Lacey, off the north side of the escarpment, is never technical but can get very fast, needing some split-second decisions about the best line to take. Climb back over the ridge to Westcott with its good bakery and bike shop, before threading your way back on easy tracks to Shere.

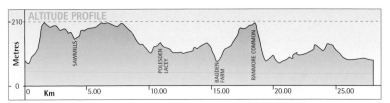

SHERE & POLESDEN LACEY		GRADE: ▲
DISTANCE: 28KM	**TOTAL ASCENT:** 400M	
START/FINISH: SHERE, JUST SOUTH OF THE A25 BETWEEN GUILDFORD & DORKING.		**GRID REFERENCE:** GR 073 480
PARKING: 'HIDDEN' CAR PARK IN SHERE. IN THE CENTRE OF VILLAGE HEAD TOWARDS ALBURY THEN TURN IMMEDIATELY RIGHT BY 30MPH SIGN ONTO TRACK NEAR THE MANOR HOUSE (GR 073 480).		
CAFÉ: LUCKY DUCK TEAROOM, SHERE Tel: 01483 202 445		
PUBLIC HOUSE: PRINCE OF WALES, SHERE Tel: 01483 202 313 or WHITE HORSE, SHERE Tel: 01483 202 518		

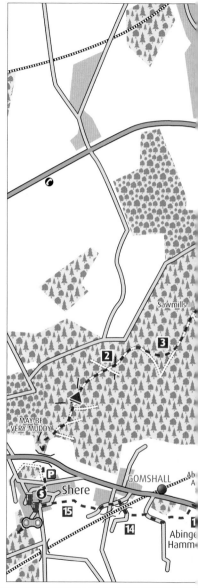

A246

0 miles 1

N

0 km 1

6

7

Polesden
Lacey

5

8

HORSE HOOF
DAMAGE

9

P

Dorking
Scout Camp

P

P

4

P

10

11

Westcott

DORKING →

12

Cricketers

A25

**Shere &
Polesden Lacey**

Directions – Shere & Polesden Lacey

➊ From the junction of Middle Street and Upper Street in Shere, turn **L** towards Albury, then immediately **R** by a *30mph* sign onto lane/track just before The Manor House. Go past the car park on the right, onto a track signposted *Byway*. The section either side of the bridge beneath the A25 is muddy after rain and rutted by 4x4s. Steep challenge. The track improves as it climbs – more flint and chalk and less mud.

2 At the X-roads of tracks at the top, continue **SA**, crossing the North Downs Way. **Ignore** a bridleway to the left. Continue **SA** around a metal barrier. At the next major track junction, by a round concrete water reservoir, continue **SA** downhill, signposted *Easy Access Route*.

3 At a T-junction, with *Combe Lane* signposted to the left, bear **R**. After 200m, as the main track swings right and climbs steeply, bear **L** onto a grass and earth track. One short rough section. At the T-junction with a broad forest road, bear **L** downhill. About 200m after passing through a timber mill surrounded by huge oak trunks, the tarmac becomes much smoother. Turn **R** gently uphill on a wide track, near a small breeze block building, signposted *Byway*.

4 Long steady climb. Pass a house on the right at the top of the climb. At a T-junction with a similar wide track, by a wooden post with red arrows, turn **L** (GR 110 496). At the X-roads with a lane by a metal barrier, go **SA**, signposted *Byway*. At the road bear **R**. Go past a lane to the left, with *6ft 6ins width limit* sign. Shortly turn **L** onto an earth and flint track, signposted *Byway*.

5 Superb, long descent, with flint and roots. The section at the bottom can be muddy after rain. Long steady climb. At the fork of tracks, shortly after the top, by a 3-way *Byway* signpost, bear **R**. The track becomes a gravel drive. Go past a parking area on the right.

6 Join tarmac near the entrance to Polesden Lacey. Use the parallel bridleway to the left. As the road swings sharp left at GR 141 533, go **SA** onto the stone track ahead, signposted *Byway*. After 800m, at the X-roads of tracks by a red poop scoop bin, turn **R**.

7 Pass beneath the power lines, then at a 3-way *Bridleway* sign at the end of the wood on the right, turn **R** onto a path running along the woodland edge. Go past a mast. Narrow between fence and trees. Fast descent. Go through two bridlegates and cross a lane **SA** onto the bridleway opposite.

8 Go past a house and barn. After 200m, as the track turns sharp left uphill, go **SA** through the gate into a field, aiming towards a solitary tree and the gate beyond. Enter woodland and bear **L** at fork. Climb steadily through woodland. Sections made rough by horses. A track joins from the right. Continue uphill.

9 At the next fork, by a wooden post with a blue arrow outlined in black (down to your left – it may be hidden by vegetation), bear **R** and keep bearing **R**. Emerge at the road, opposite a red tile-clad house and turn **R***. Climb, descend, then at the top of the second climb, turn **L** onto a wide stone track, towards a metal barrier with a *Dorking Scout Council* sign.

*If the road is busy you may prefer to use the verge-side tracks on either side of the road.

10 Go past the scout camp on your left. At a X-roads with the North Downs Way, continue **SA**, signposted *Byway*. Good descent. At a X-roads with a wide earth track at the bottom, continue **SA**. Cross the railway line, join tarmac and continue in the same direction.

11 At the T-junction, opposite a house called The Mill, turn **R** on Balchins Lane – or for the bakery, The Cricketers pub and Nirvana bike shop in Westcott, turn **L**. After 600m take the first lane **R*** ▶OR▷ , signposted *Wotton Estate/Bridleway*. Shortly, **ignore** the first right at a 4-way signpost. Take the next **R** at a 3-way signpost, opposite a telegraph pole on the left.

* ▶OR▷ for link to **Abinger & Leith Hill** ride go **SA**.

12 At the offset X-roads of tracks, with a house ahead, turn **L** then **R**, signposted *Bridleway*, to go past an old brick & wood barn. At the road, turn **L** then **R**, onto a continuation of the bridleway. **Ignore** several turns to right and left. At the road, with a footpath ahead, turn **L** downhill.

13 At the T-junction with the A25, turn **R**. After 200m, opposite the double wooden gates at the end of a magnificent old brick and timber house, turn **L** onto a broad gravel bridleway. Gravel turns to concrete. Shortly after crossing a stream, with Brook Cottage ahead, bear **L** onto a parallel earth track, signposted *Bridleway*.

DIRECTIONS CONTINUE ON NEXT PAGE

14 At a T-junction with a wide gravel drive, turn **R**. After 250m, as the gravel track swings right, turn **L** on the second of two closely spaced tracks to the left. This is a narrow earth bridleway (blue arrow) that passes alongside a fence to the right. At the T-junction beyond the farm, turn **R** under the railway bridge, then immediately at the next T-junction, turn **L**.

15 Take the first road **R**, signposted *Guildford*, then go **SA** onto Gravelpits Lane, signposted *Bridleway*. Turn **R** by Gravelpits Farmhouse (blue arrow). At the junction with tarmac, go **SA**, then at the T-junction with Shere Lane, turn **R** to return to the start.

◄⚙═◎ **Making a day of it**

This ride overlaps with two others. For the best way of zipping together this ride with the **Shalford & Albury** ride *(see page 18)*. For a link to the **Abinger & Leith Hill** ride *(see page 29)* follow this ride from Instruction **1** to the start of Instruction **11** then join the **Leith Hill** ride at Instruction **2** *("...At the T-junction with the busy A25...")*

4 Abinger & Leith Hill

24km

Introduction

Leith Hill is not only the highest point in South East England, at a mighty 294m/965ft, but also a big draw for mountain bikers, as the area is criss-crossed with byways and bridleways. It also features 'Summer Lightning', a waymarked singletrack ride on Forestry Commission land, and you will come across signs for it as you follow this ride. The ascent of the south face of Holmbury Hill is extraordinarily steep, more like a mountain scramble than a hill, but it sets you up for a long, gentle descent towards Peaslake.

The Ride

A gentle warm-up from the car park to Westcott is followed by one of the longest climbs on the North Downs – over 210m/700ft – taking you on sandy woodland tracks up to Leith Hill Tower. Enjoy a weekend feast at the café and great views all year round, before the long descent to the B2126. Get your crampons, ice axe and harness ready for the assault on Holmbury Hill, then glide down through woodland and narrow tracks to Peaslake and Abinger Hammer.

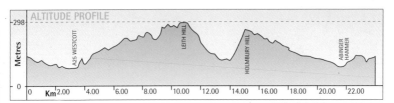

ABINGER & LEITH HILL	GRADE: ▲

DISTANCE: 24KM

TOTAL ASCENT: 400M

START/FINISH: ABINGER ROUGHS CAR PARK, ON THE MINOR LANE LEADING NORTH TOWARDS EFFINGHAM OFF THE A25 BETWEEN GOMSHALL AND WESTCOTT (OPPOSITE RAIKES LANE). **GRID REFERENCE:** GR 111 481

PARKING: AS ABOVE AT GR 111 481

CAFÉ: ABINGER TEAROOMS, ABINGER Tel: 01306 730 811
CAFE OPEN AT LEITH HILL TOWER AT THE WEEKENDS

PUBLIC HOUSE: ABINGER ARMS, ABINGER Tel: 01306 711 793. PLOUGH INN, COLDHARBOUR Tel: 01306 711 793

Dorking

Cricketers

Westcott

A25

'Summer
Lightning'

Plough
Inn

Coldharbour

Holmbury
Hill

Leith Hill
Tower

Joldwynds

Abinger & Leith Hill

Directions – Abinger & Leith Hill

➊ Exit the car park (GR 111 481) and turn **L**. Climb, then start descending. Shortly after a *Horse* road sign (red triangle), turn **R**, signposted *Bridleway*. At a major junction beyond an old brick barn, go **SA**, following the line of telegraph poles. At the T-junction, with a telegraph pole in the wooden fence ahead, bear **L**.

2 At the T-junction, with a row of houses to the left, turn **R**. At the T-junction with the busy A25, turn **L** then **R** onto Rookery Drive (**take care**). Follow the road round to the right past Mill House, then just before the high hedges of The Rookery, turn **L** onto a sandy track signposted *Bridleway*.

3 How far can you climb without a dab? At the T-junction with a wider track, turn **L** to continue uphill, signposted *Byway*. At the obvious fork, take either track (they rejoin). Steady climb over 3.5km, at times damaged by 4x4s and scramble bikes.

4 At the junction with the road by the Plough Inn in Coldharbour, turn **R** uphill, signposted *Byway*, onto a wide gravel track and shortly fork **R**, signposted *Tower*. Steep climb. At the fork by the cricket ground, bear **L**. After 800m at a X-roads of tracks with a post with red arrows to the left and a green-topped post to the right, turn **R** downhill. Climb, then shortly after the start of the descent you come to a mega-junction of tracks. Turn **L** steeply uphill by a 4-way signpost towards Leith Hill Tower.

5 Go past the tower and continue in the same direction – west – descending towards Starveall Corner car park. Keep following a 'Car' icon with an 'S' in it. At the T-junction with the road, turn **L**. When you come to the end of verge-side parking on the right, turn **R**, signposted *Bridleway, Greensand Way*. Keep bearing **L** to continue downhill.

6 At a path junction by a house called The Coach House, go **SA** on the bridleway. Shortly, with a locked gate across the main track, turn **L** over a small bridge onto a parallel track. This becomes narrow along the field edge. At the road, turn **L** downhill for 250m then turn **R** onto the bridleway – not the footpath before this. Emerge at the road at the top of a climb by a house called Joldwynds and turn **L**.

7 **Easy to miss**: shortly after a big house on the bend (Holmbury House) keep an eye out for a narrow track to the **R**, signposted *Bridleway*, before a small garage – also on the right. At the top of an exceedingly steep climb, turn **L** towards the monument. Pass to the **L** of the concrete donation box, signposted *Bridleway* (white arrow on black circle).

8 Bear **L** at three forks of tracks. By avoiding the *Footpath only* tracks, you will soon arrive at a major junction of tracks with a pond to the left. Go **SA** towards a stone/concrete *Hurtwood Millennium Pinetum* cairn. Turn **R** just before the cairn, on a gently descending wide gravel track (heading NNE).

9 **Easy to miss**: after 800m of fast descent, you come to a X-roads of tracks in a clearing, with two tracks climbing steeply to the left. Turn **L** uphill, by a lonesome Scots pine, onto the second of these tracks (GR 103 441). Short steep climb, long gentle descent, **ignoring** turnings to left and right.

10 At a T-junction, with a grand house ahead, bear **R**. Some muddy sections, a few badger setts. Join tarmac and continue downhill. At the T-junction at the end of Franksfield, bear **R** uphill (in effect **SA**). At the T-junction at the end of Hoe Lane, turn **R**. After 450m, immediately after a telephone box on the left, turn **R** onto Rad Lane (no through road). Shortly, turn **L** onto a broad gravel track, signposted *Bridleway*.

11 Ever-better downhill with yellow sandbanks from badger setts. At the bottom, at a T-junction with a concrete track, turn **R**. At the T-junction with the busy A25, turn **R**, then take the first road **L** by Abinger Arms pub onto a no through road, just before the ornate clocktower on the building ahead.

12 At the top of the climb, turn **R**, signposted *Bridleway*. Short section along a narrow field edge path with fence to the left, then much longer, wider, attractive track undulating through woodland. At the road turn **R** to return to the start.

←⊙⊙ Making a day of it

There is a 4km overlap between this ride and the **Shere & Polesden Lacey** ride. To link the two in one big ride *(see page 26)*. It also touches the **Shalford & Albury** ride at Abinger Hammer *(see page 13)*.

5 Reigate Hill, Stane Street, Box Hill

30km

Introduction

Strange though it may seem, Reigate would be the perfect base for exploring most of the rides in this book – an hour's drive east and west covers most of the North Downs rides and an hour south takes you to Brighton and the South Downs. And let's not forget the quality of the rides right on the doorstep. This one from Reigate Hill has all the right ingredients – a good café in the (free) car park at the start and a mixture of well-maintained, well-sign-posted broad and narrow tracks up and down through the wooded countryside, that belies your proximity to the zillions of good Surrey citizens living nearby.

The Ride

Leave the car park and follow the North Downs Way westward, with panoramic views out over the Mole Valley. The section across the open grasslands and broadleaf woodland of Banstead Heath takes you to Walton on the Hill and the one incongruous suburban street along the whole ride. This is soon forgotten on the splendid bit of downhill singletrack to Nohome Farm. Join the old Roman road of Stane Street and enjoy the rollercoaster descent down to Mickleham. A long steady climb up through Box Hill Country Park leads to a plateau section through the woodlands of Headley Heath, before rejoining the North Downs Way past opulent mansions, to return for coffee and cakes at the start.

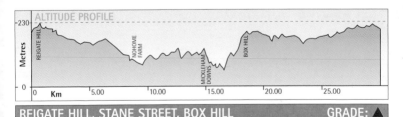

ALTITUDE PROFILE

REIGATE HILL, STANE STREET, BOX HILL   GRADE: ▲

DISTANCE: 30KM   **TOTAL ASCENT:** 300M

START/FINISH: REIGATE HILL CAR PARK – FROM M25 JCT 8 FOLLOW SIGNS FOR 'REIGATE' THEN 'MERSTHAM' THEN 'PARKING & VIEWPOINT' (BROWN & WHITE SIGNS)

GRID REFERENCE: GR 262 523

PARKING: SEE ABOVE. GR 262 523

CAFÉ: CAFÉ AT THE START/FINISH

PUBLIC HOUSE: BLUE BALL, WALTON ON THE HILL Tel: 01737 812 168

BANSTEAD

N

0 miles   1

0 km   1

Tadworth

Kingswood

4

Blue Ball

3

Banstead
Heath

P

B2032

2

P

Junction 8

M25

14

15

Reigate
Hill

S

P

North Downs Way

A217

Redhill

Reigate

**Reigate Hill, Stane
Street, Box Hill**

Directions – Reigate Hill, Stone Street, Box Hill

➊ From the car park, cross the footbridge over the A217 to the **L** of the café. Continue in the same direction, on gravel (and, briefly, tarmac) going past masts to your right, then a temple/monument to your left. Cross a large open grassy area with huge views to the left. Re-enter woodland, then immediately after a tall red-brick tower on the right, turn **R** through a bridlegate to cross the bridge over the M25.

➋ Go through wood and car park. At the road, bear **L** onto a track beyond white metal bollards, signposted *Bridleway*. Track turns to tarmac. Shortly, at a X-roads (your priority) with a shop to the left, turn **L** onto a track, signposted *Bridleway*, immediately beyond Mogador Road to the left, alongside a wooden fence.

➌ After 1km, pass to the **L** of a *Banstead Commons Conservators* board. Follow signs for *Dorking Road, Bridleway* at the next junction. Continue in the same direction at X-roads of tracks (muddy after rain), eventually bearing **L** at a 3-way *Dorking Road, Bridleway* sign. At X-roads with B2032, go **SA**, signposted *Bridleway*.

➍ Bear **L** as houses appear on the left. Emerge at Blue Ball pub and the pond in Walton on the Hill. Turn **L** on Walton Street, then at the end of the pond, turn **R** onto Sandlands Road. At the T-junction at the end of the road, turn **L** onto a wide gravel path, signposted *Byway*. At the road, turn **R** then shortly bear **L**, aiming for the enclosed drive/bridleway that leads to The Cotton Mills to the **L** of a *Hurst Road* sign.

➎ Superb singletrack, then woodland descent. Emerge by Nohome Farm and turn **L** on a broad earth and gravel track. Join tarmac, go through farm. At the T-junction with the busy road, turn **L** uphill on an excellent parallel bridleway.

➏ At the end of the parallel track, go **SA** to cross the road onto the bridleway ahead, joining Shepherd's Walk (no through road). Turn **L**. Fast gravel descent. At the fork, bear **L**, signposted *No cars, no motorbikes*. Keep following signs for *Stane Street, Mickleham*.

7 Cross the M25. Cross two minor roads. Fast descent to cross a busier road (B2033, golf course to left) and go **SA** uphill. Whoop de whoop! Second short dip. At the bottom of the third dip, shortly after a footpath sign to *Givons Grove* to your right, you come to a fork of tracks. Bear **R** downhill on the lower track, by a *Downs Road, Mickleham 1 mile* signpost.

8 **Ignore** turns to right and left, following *Thamesdown Link* purple arrows. At the T-junction with the road, with a low red-brick wall ahead, turn **L**. After 550m, turn **R** into Whitehill car park, following the obvious bridleway. Steady then steep climb.

9 At the T-junction with the road, by a bar called Smith & Western, turn **L**. After 1km, and shortly after passing Box Hill village hall and a small modern church on your right, take the next road to the **L**, signposted *High Ashurst, Bridleway*.

10 **Easy to miss**: after 750m, immediately after a road joins from the right, by ornate wooden gates, brick pillars and carved figures, you come to a broad track, signposted *National Trust, Headley Heath*. Turn **R** here and follow the main track as it descends then climbs. **Ignore** a left turn by wooden barriers, as the main track continues **R** uphill.

11 At the top of a short climb at an obvious T-junction by a low round wooden post, turn **L** then **R**, to continue in the same direction. Shortly at a T-junction with a similar broad track, bear **L**. At the junction with the B2032 at Headley Heath car park, go **SA** on a track to the right of Wardens Cottage drive.

12 At the X-roads with tarmac, with a house called *White Lodge* to the right, go **SA** on a narrow track. Shortly, at the T-junction, turn **R** by a *National Trust Headley Heath* sign. Fast descent under a dark canopy of vegetation. As the track starts to climb, at a fork by a 2-way blue arrow near a holly tree, bear **R**.

13 At the X-roads with the busy B2032, go **SA**, signposted *Bridleway*. At the T-junction with a wire fence and a field ahead, turn **L**. At the T-junction with a wide track, turn **R**, signposted *Byway*. **Easy to miss**: after 600m, at a 4-way signpost, shortly after the start of the steep descent, bear **L** uphill off the main track.

DIRECTIONS CONTINUE ON NEXT PAGE

Directions – Reigate Hill, Stane Street, Box Hill Continued

14 Emerge from woodland. At the end of the field to your left, turn **L** steeply uphill on a wide gravel and stone track. (Straight ahead is a rough, muddy and narrow track.)

15 Go **SA** at several X-roads, including a 'corridor' section between wooden fences. Opposite a house called *Mole Place* to the right and a sign ahead saying *Steep hill, cyclists advised to dismount*, turn **L** on tarmac, then second **R** by tall metal bollards and a 4-way *Bridleway* sign. Rejoin the outward route to return to the start.

◄◘◘◘ Making a day of it

The best connection to the next ride to the west (**Abinger & Leith Hill**, *page 29*) would either be from Mickleham and Westhumble towards Polesden Lacey, or from the fork of tracks at the start of Stane Street via Leatherhead and Fetcham Downs. To the east, following a mixture of the North Downs Way on its bridleway sections and connecting minor lanes through Gatton and to the north of Merstham links you to the **Godstone** ride *(page 43)* at Gravelly Hill.

6 Godstone & Oxted

Introduction

There are a couple of spooky things about this ride along the sand and chalk tracks between Oxted and Caterham: shortly after leaving Godstone there is a gate that mysteriously opens by itself... then later, as you pass by Barrow Green Court, your every move is scrutinised by loads of security cameras just before the bridge over the M25. Don't be put off, this ride has enough fine woodland tracks, challenging climbs and fun descents to overcome fears of being spied upon.

The Ride

A short tarmac warm-up south from Godstone takes you to the start of the first off-road section. As ever in these parts, this is a series of short stretches of track that can be linked together to form rides that are definitely better second and third time around when you don't have your head buried in the map or guidebook. Bypass Oxted and climb steeply after crossing the M25. How far can you climb without a dab? Enjoy the views from high up on the North Downs before dropping fast on good woodland tracks on Gravelly Hill and around the sand pit. Beer in Bletchingley? The last off-road section wanders through woods and past paddocks before a fast tarmac descent to Godstone.

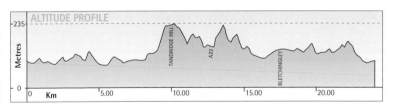

ALTITUDE PROFILE

235 Metres — TANDRIDGE HILL — A22 — BLETCHINGLEY

0

0 Km   5.00   10.00   15.00   20.00

GODSTONE & OXTED   GRADE: ▲

DISTANCE: 24KM

TOTAL ASCENT: 400M

START/FINISH: GODSTONE, EAST OF REIGATE

GRID REFERENCE: GR 350 516

PARKING: BY THE POND AND AROUND THE GREEN NEAR THE WHITE HART PUB (GR 350 516)

CAFÉ: GODSTONE SANDWICH BAR Tel: 01883 742 946

PUBLIC HOUSE: WHITE HART, GODSTONE Tel: 01883 742 521. OLD BELL, OXTED Tel: 01883 741 877.
PRINCE ALBERT, BLETCHINGLEY Tel: 01883 743 257, WHYTE HART, BLETCHINGLEY Tel: 01883 743 231.

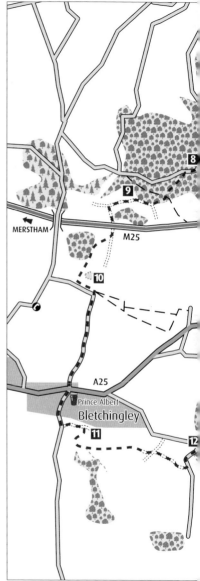

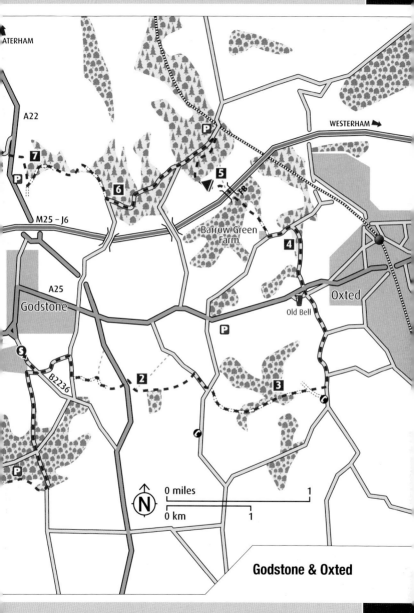

ATERHAM

A22

7

P

M25 – J6

A25

Godstone

S

B2236

2

WESTERHAM ➤

P

6

5

F8

Barrow Green Farm

4

Oxted

Old Bell

P

3

0 miles 1

(N)

0 km 1

P

Godstone & Oxted

Directions – Godstone & Oxted

➔ With your back to the White Hart pub in Godstone (by the pond), turn **L** towards The Bell pub. At the end of the last houses on the left, immediately after the *40mph speed limit* signs, take the first lane **L**, signposted *6ft 6ins width limit*. Climb then descend. At the T-junction at the end of Bull Beggars Lane, turn **R**. After 250m, on a descent, take the first lane to the **L**: a no through road signposted *Bridleway, Leigh Place*.

2 Tarmac turns to track. Pass through underpass and at the T-junction by Hop Garden Cottage, turn **R**, soon joining an improved gravel path. At the T-junction with the road, by a house called *The Dairy*, turn **R**. At the T-junction at the end of Jackass Lane, turn **L** then **R** onto a tarmac drive signposted *Farm Shop, Bridleway*.

3 Follow the tarmac drive to the end, where it becomes track. Pass beneath a footbridge and climb under a dark evergreen canopy. At the road, bear **R** downhill. Continue in the same direction at the next road junction, **SA** onto bridleway. At T-junction with a wider road, near to *30mph* signs, turn **L**. Climb then descend.

4 At X-roads by the Old Bell pub in Oxted, go **SA** onto Brook Hill. At the T-junction at the end of Sandy Lane, turn **L**. Descend, climb, and start descending again. Take the first tarmac drive on the **R**, signposted *Barrow Green Farmhouse* (low *Bridleway* stone marker). Security cameras everywhere. Cross the M25 bridge and bear **L** to continue uphill on a narrow fenced track.

5 Steep climb with some roots. How far can you go without a dab? At the T-junction with a broader track by a *North Downs Way/Woldingham Countryside Walk* signpost, turn **L*** steeply uphill. Turn **L** again, just before the road, signposted *North Downs Way* (blue arrow). Join road and bear **L**.

*If you come to wooden benches at a viewpoint, you have gone 50m too far. Retrace.

6 **Easy to miss**: **ignore** the first road to the left, climb, descend and go round a **LH** bend. Cross the North Downs Way, then as the gradient steepens, on a second **LH** bend, turn sharp **R** back on yourself, signposted *Bridleway*, onto a wide track/lane. At a T-junction with a barrier and a *Private* road sign to the right, turn **L** on the North Downs Way (blue arrow).

7 Track turns to concrete then tarmac. Follow the road **L** downhill past Spaceworks factory. **Easy to miss**: shortly after the factory, on a **LH** bend on the descent, turn **R**

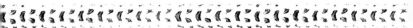

sharply back on yourself, travelling uphill on a wide gravel track, signposted *National Cycle Network Route 21 (NCN 21), Bridleway*. At the T-junction with the A22 dual carriageway, turn **L** on the cyclepath, cross the bridge then bear **L** steeply uphill on lane.

8 Immediately after the Downs Residential Site turn **L** on a track by metal bollards (stone *Bridleway* marker). At the T-junction with a better track, bear **R** gently uphill, signposted *North Downs Way* (blue arrow). At the T-junction with the road by Caterham Viewpoint, turn **L**. Bear **L** shortly, signposted *NCN 21, North Downs Way* (blue arrow).

9 At the fork, bear **L** to continue downhill, signposted *NCN 21* (the North Downs Way footpath is to your right). Shortly, at the X-roads of tracks, bear **R**, signposted *NCN 21* (blue arrow). Keep following *NCN 21* signs, eventually turning **L*** at a X-roads of tracks with a small rickety shed in the field on the left (GR 332 529). Go under M25.

*If you hit tarmac and a see a drive on the left to White Hill House you have come 100m too far. Retrace.

10 At T-junction with road, turn **L** and follow round a **RH** bend. At X-roads with the busy A25 in Bletchingley, go **SA** onto Outwood Lane. After 450m, at the end of houses, turn **L** by *50mph* speed signs, then immediately **L** again, signposted *Bridleway*.

11 Go past the pond, then just after the top of the climb, turn **R** downhill on a narrow track towards the field, between two concrete posts. At first rough. Continue **SA** downhill on a narrow track at a X-roads of tracks with a locked metal gate to the right. Soon join a fine, level track.

12 At the T-junction with the road, bear **L** uphill, then shortly bear **R**, signposted *Bridleway*, onto a wide gravel track. At the road, turn **L** uphill for 200m then keep an eye out for a *Bridleway* sign to the **R**. At the T-junction with road, turn **L**. Climb then descend. At the T-junction with the old A22, turn **L** to return to Godstone.

← Making a day of it

From the northwest corner of this ride (Gravelly Hill) it is possible to use a combination of the North Downs Way, where it is bridleway, and minor lanes to the north of Merstham and through Gatton to link to the **Reigate Hill** ride *(page 35)*.

7 Ightham & Mereworth Woods 25km

Introduction

Any good at riding up steps? There is an odd set of steps carved into the steep track that leads west of Ightham up to the old Iron Age hill fort of Oldbury Hill. You soon know you are in Kent, Garden of England, as you cross apple orchards, a riot of blossom in the springtime. This ride even features a bit of culture in the form of the beautiful old buildings at Ightham Mote, which also has a café attached. But surely the most remarkable section of the ride is the long bridleway through the sweet chestnut coppices of Mereworth Woods.

The Ride

Head west from Ightham on a winding route to maximise time on the sandy tracks around Oldbury Hill and Raspit Hill. This contrasts with the next part of the ride through orchards, past the estates and neat countryside around Ightham Mote and Fairlawne. The third element in the ride is the long woodland section through Mereworth Woods, a place that you could imagine to be full of dark secrets.

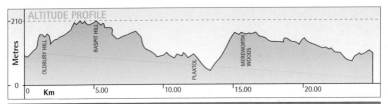

ALTITUDE PROFILE

Metres — 210 — 0

OLDBURY HILL — RASPIT HILL — PLAXTOL — MEREWORTH WOODS

0 — Km — 5.00 — 10.00 — 15.00 — 20.00

IGHTHAM & MEREWORTH WOODS — GRADE: ▲

DISTANCE: 25KM

START/FINISH: IGHTHAM, ON THE A227/A25 EAST OF SEVENOAKS

PARKING: IGHTHAM VILLAGE HALL CAR PARK (GR 594 566)

TOTAL ASCENT: 300M

GRID REFERENCE: GR 594 566

CAFÉ: IGHTHAM MOTE (CLOSED TUE & SAT) Tel: 01732 810 378

PUBLIC HOUSE: CHEQUERS, IGHTHAM Tel: 01732 882 396. PAPERMAKERS ARMS, PLAXTOL Tel: 01732 810 407.
GEORGE & DRAGON, IGHTHAM Tel: 01732 882 440. PADWELL ARMS, STONE STREET Tel: 01732 761 532.
OLD BEECH INN, B2016, MEREWORTH WOODS Tel: 01622 813 038.

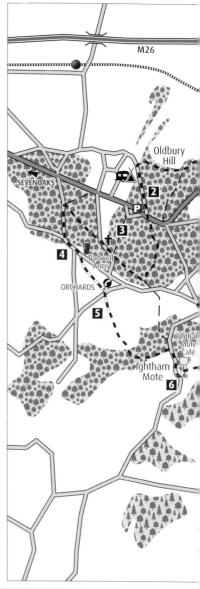

M26 JC2a **MAIDSTONE**

Ightham

15

14

Sotts Hole
Cottage

13

12

B2016

11

MEREWORTH
WOODS

10

Old Beech Inn

Plaxtol

7 Fairlawne

8

Papermakers
Arms

9

A227

ONBRIDGE

N

0 miles 1

0 km 1

Ightham &
Mereworth Woods

Directions – Ightham &
Mereworth Woods

➊ Turn **R** out of Ightham village hall car park onto Sevenoaks Road. At the X-roads with the A25, go **SA** (**take care**) onto Oldbury Lane. Climb past school and continue in the same direction, as the lane becomes a no through road. Continue **SA** towards a *No parking, no turning* sign. Pass to the **R** of the garage onto grass, signposted *Bridleway* (on a stone marker). Very steep woodland climb with steps.

2 At the junction of tracks by *Oldbury Hill* signboard, bear **R** downhill and keep bearing **R**. At the T-junction with the road at the bottom of the descent, turn **L** (by Styants Farm House). At the X-roads with the A25, turn **L** then **R**, signposted *Bridleway* (**take care**).

3 Very fine woodland track with some sandy sections. At the T-junction at the top of steps, turn **R** onto a track that has been improved with road scrapings. Muddy after rain. Follow in same direction for 1km. There are many tracks and forks, several of which rejoin. Emerge at road and bear **R** past school and church. On a **RH** bend, bear **L** on a bridleway leading into woodland. Continue in the same direction for 1km (there are many track junctions).

4 At the T-junction with the road, turn **L** downhill. At the T-junction with a wider road by a *Give Way* sign, turn **L**. After 300m, turn **R** opposite the Padwell Arms pub onto a wide gravel track (the *Bridleway* sign is half-hidden in the hedge).

5 Pass through orchards. At a 5-way junction of roads, go **SA** onto the narrow lane, signposted *Bridleway*. Keep to the **R** of orchard, then continue in the same direction downhill as the track narrows and steepens. Cleared woodland at the bottom. Follow the stream downhill.

6 At the T-junction with the road, turn **R**. Follow the boundary of Ightham Mote to your left. Turn sharp **L** between brick pillars opposite the end of the red-brick barn of Mote Farm on the right, signposted *Ightham Mote, Bridleway*.

7   Go past Ightham Mote.* At the gate at the end of the enclosed section, turn **R** (blue arrow) along the field edge. Exit the field via bridlegate and turn **L** along a wide stone track. Go **SA** at the busy A227 (**take care**) through a bridlegate opposite, into Fairlawne Estate. At the tarmac T-junction, turn **L** then shortly **R**, following *Bridlepath* signs. Go into a field via a bridlegate.

    *The entrance to Ightam Mote café is through the car park on the **L** beyond the main house.

8   Follow the obvious grass track through the estate past many magnificent trees. At the T-junction with the road, turn **L** then after 300m first **R** onto The Street. Go downhill through Plaxtol past the Papermakers Arms. **Ignore** a right turn to Dunk Green by a telephone box. Take the next **R** on Brook Lane towards Old Soar Manor.

9   At the T-junction with Allens Lane, turn **L**. As the road swings sharp left and becomes Old Soar Road, bear **R** (in effect **SA**) onto a track (no sign). **Ignore** a wide gravel track on the right and continue in the same direction uphill on a narrower track.

10   Long climb. At the T-junction with a similar track turn **L** uphill. At the road junction, go **SA** onto the bridleway opposite. At a X-roads with a broad track (footpath), go **SA** (blue arrow). Amazing coppiced sweet chestnut woodland. Continue in the same direction for 2.2km. At the X-roads with the fast and busy B2016, go **SA** (Old Beech Inn to your right).

11   **Easy to miss**: after 150m, opposite New Pound Lane to the right, turn **L** onto a narrow track between hedges, beyond a metal barrier. Go **SA** at two X-roads of tracks. At the next junction, with a metal fence to the left, as the main track swings right, bear **L** (in effect **SA**). After 400m keep an eye out for a double telegraph pole with a metal transformer to the left. Turn sharp **L** here on a narrow track to go past red-brick Longwall House.

12   Emerge at the B2016, turn **R** then **L** after 20m, opposite the next house, onto a narrow woodland path signposted *Bridleway*. Follow the obvious earth track. After 1km join a wide forest road on a U-bend. Bear **R**.

DIRECTIONS CONTINUE ON NEXT PAGE

13 After 750m, shortly after the second **LH** bend at the bottom of a gentle descent and about 20m **before** a *Hurst Wood* sign, turn **R** sharply back on yourself by a wooden field gate. Go past new executive houses. At the junction with The Old Saw Mill, turn **L** opposite the street sign, onto a narrow track signposted *Bridleway* (stone marker).

14 At the T-junction with the road, turn **L** then **R** on to Crouch Lane towards Borough Green. **Easy to miss**: at the bottom of a dip, shortly after the tarmac drive of Sotts Hole Cottage, turn **L** down steps to join the bridleway that runs parallel to the drive. Descend steeply. At the road junction by houses, turn **L** then **R** onto Mill Lane.

15 Climb. At the offset X-roads of lanes, turn **L** then **R** to cross a bridge. At the T-junction with the A227, turn **R** then shortly **L** onto Sevenoaks Road to return to Ightham village hall car park.

◄O Making a day of it

Following the minor road for 3km due north of Ightham, past Ightham Court, links you to the south west corner of the **Wrotham** ride *(see page 57)* at GR 593 596.

8 Wrotham & the North Downs Way

35km

Introduction

Coldrum Longbarrow is certainly one of the highlights of this ride – a ring of atmospheric stones looking down over the lush Kent countryside. Another feature is the top grade quality of much of the North Downs Way where, from spring to autumn, you will feel like you are gliding through a green tunnel under a canopy of vegetation. As this ride consists of many sections of byways, bridleways and quiet lanes bolted together to maximise off-road content, it may feel bitty first time round. Do it a second and third time and it will all fall more naturally into place.

The Ride

Cross the busy A20 above the even busier M20 and escape onto Pilgrims' Way (folks heading for Canterbury, way back when). Make the effort to divert to see Kent's own mini Stonehenge at Coldrum Longbarrow, before returning to the North Downs Way past cliffs of chalk from old quarries and up into Great Park Wood. Our friends, the 4x4 boys, may have trashed some of the plateau sections. Wiggle your way through to the pub at Harvel, this time with the odd curse aimed at horse hoof damage. Turn west then south after the windmill at Meopham Green, heading through strips of woodland, and on quiet lanes to a testing singletrack descent after the M20 bridge crossing and a great smooth finish on the North Downs Way.

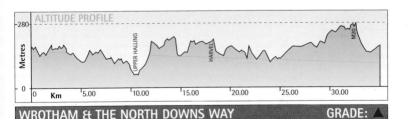

ALTITUDE PROFILE

Metres — 280 — 0

UPPER HALLING   HARVEL   M20

Km   0   5.00   10.00   15.00   20.00   25.00   30.00

WROTHAM & THE NORTH DOWNS WAY

GRADE: ▲

DISTANCE: 35KM

TOTAL ASCENT: 450M

START/FINISH: WROTHAM, EAST OF SEVENOAKS

GRID REFERENCE: GR 611 592

PARKING: ON WEST STREET, NEAR CHURCH IN WROTHAM. GR 611 592   **CAFÉ:** BRING SANDWICHES

PUBLIC HOUSE: LOTS OF CHOICE IN WROTHAM. AMAZON & TIGER, HARVEL. LONG HOP, KINGS ARMS, MEOPHAM GREEN. ANCHOR & HOPE, SOUTH OF ASH

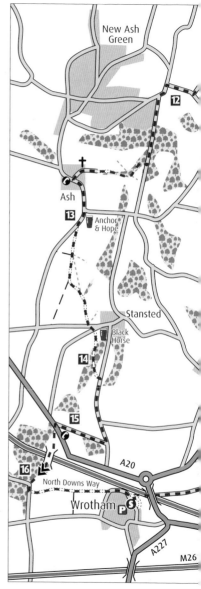

GRAVESEND

11

Meopham Green

A227

10

Upper
Halling

6

POTENTIALLY
VERY MUDDY

5

9

Harvel

HORSE
HOOF
DAMAGE

Amazon
& Tiger

Asvins

Lad's
Farm

8

7

Culverstone
Green

4

Snodland

Vigo

Pilgrims' Way

Coldrum
Longbarrow

3

2

Pilgrims' Way

Birling

20

Trottiscliffe

MAIDSTONE ➡

M20

Wrotham & the North
Downs Way

Directions – Wrotham & the North Downs Way

➎ Turn **R** out of the car park on West Street in Wrotham. At the T-junction by the Three Post Boys, turn **L** and climb on a no through road past public conveniences. Opposite the playground to the left, turn **R** by recycling bins, signposted *North Downs Way*, onto a narrow tarmac path. Cross the busy A20 onto the pavement opposite and turn **L**. Just before the roundabout turn **R** onto the lane called Pilgrims' Way.

2 Descend, climb, descend. At the top of the second climb, as the road turns sharp right downhill, bear **L** (in effect **SA**), signposted *Byway*. Shortly, at a fork of byways, bear **R** on the lower track. Fine surface track through a green 'tunnel' of vegetation.

3 At the road, turn **R** then **L** onto no through road, signposted *Pilgrims' Way*. After 1.3km, take the first road **R** (Pinesfield Lane). After 600m descending gently, turn **L**, signposted *Coldrum Longbarrow car park*. Go past the car park; round a gate and along a field edge. At the junction of tracks with *Coldrum Longbarrow* signposted to the right (worth a visit), turn **L** sharply back on yourself. Short steep climb. At junction with tarmac, turn **R** then bear **R** onto the bridleway.

4 Fine smooth track. **Ignore** turns to left and right. At low wooden barriers, continue **SA**, signposted *North Downs Way* (blue arrow). Smooth track – maybe muddy in winter. At the T-junction with road, turn **L** then **R** on continuation of track. The track narrows. At the junction with tarmac immediately after a green metal barrier, continue **SA**.

5 At the next T-junction, bear **L** (in effect **SA**), by Lad's Farm. At the X-roads in the village of Upper Halling, turn **L** uphill on Chapel Lane by an old brick and flint house with red tiles. Tarmac turns to track as the gradient steepens. With a metal barrier ahead, follow the wide stone track sharply round to the **R**.

6 After reaching the top there will be mud after rain. At the T-junction with a similar wide stone and earth track, turn **L** uphill (no sign, pylon in the field to your left). First section is muddy after rain. At the track junction by four round green metal bollards, turn **R** downhill. Steep descent. At the T-junction with the road at the bottom, with a large new brick house ahead, turn **L**, passing a converted chapel to your right.

7 Tarmac turns to unmetalled road by a house called Valley View. At the turning area near tall metal fencing on the left, turn **R** by metal posts and a wooden barrier onto a field edge path (blue arrow). Climb towards woodland – first 400m very badly damaged by horses, but gets better at the top.

8 Follow good path round **RH** bend then at the T-junction with the road by Leywood Schoolhouse, turn **L**. After 100m, turn **R** onto a bridleway. At the T-junction with tarmac, with a black and white timbered house ahead, turn **L**.

9 Turn **R** at the T-junction, with Harvel village green to the right. **Ignore** turns to right and left through Harvel. **Easy to miss**: about 500m after the Amazon & Tiger pub, take the next **L** on Heron Hill Lane, signposted *Byway*. Go round **RH** and **LH** bends on a good quality track. Steep descent. Emerge from wood, join tarmac. At the top of the climb, turn **R** on a wide, improved track (red arrow) opposite a house called Asvins.

10 At a flint-and-tile-clad house, follow the track round to the **R** – there is a *Private road* sign ahead. At the fork of roads by the village green in Meopham Green, bear **R**. At the T-junction with the A227, turn **R**. After 300m, opposite Meopham Village Hall, turn **L** at the end of the houses on the left, onto a tarmac lane and through a wooden gate into a field.

11 At the second field, follow the **LH** field edge. Descend then climb through a small patch of woodland and through a metal gate into a third field. Aim for the **RH** edge of the woodland ahead. At a T-junction with a wide grassy track, by a wooden post with yellow and blue arrows, turn **R**, signposted *Bridleway*. At the junction with the road turn **L**.

12 At the T-junction, turn **R** signposted *New Ash Green*. At the next T-junction, turn **L** (same sign), then shortly first **L**, signposted *Ridley*. **Easy to miss**: after 900m, keep an eye out for a narrow track to the **R** by two metal bollards, signposted *No cars, no motorbikes*.

13 Join tarmac, soon passing a large old red-brick house and a flint and brick church in Ash. At the T-junction at the end of Church Road, turn **L**. About 250m after passing the Anchor & Hope pub, on a **RH** bend, bear **L** onto a narrow earth and stone track, signposted *Byway. No cars, no motorbikes*. Fine track through woodland.

DIRECTIONS CONTINUE ON NEXT PAGE

14 At the T-junction with the road, turn **L**. (Oak Tree Farm is on the left.) At the T-junction with Plaxdale Green Road, turn **R** then **L** onto a narrow track, signposted *Byway, No cars, no motorbikes*. Descend then climb, at first steeply then more gently. At the T-junction with tarmac by Stansted Lodge Farm, turn **R**.

15 **Ignore** a left to Fairseat. With a no through road ahead, follow the road round a sharp **RH** bend. At the T-junction with the A20, turn **L** then **R** onto bridleway (**take care**). Go through the heaviest gate in the world! Continue **SA**, passing to the right of a line of oaks, towards a metal gate and across the bridge over the M20. Huge views.

16 Great descent with the odd testing section. At the road, turn **L** downhill, then shortly **L** onto a fine gravel track (North Downs Way). The track turns to tarmac. At the X-roads, go **SA** onto a continuation of Pilgrims' Way/North Downs Way then follow this road back to the car park in Wrotham.

←🔗 Making a day of it

Wrotham lies close to Ightham *(see page 49)*. The rides could be linked via the minor lane that heads south from the crossing of the M25, near the end of the ride, to the west of Wrotham.

9 Chilham & King's Wood

23km

Introduction

King's Wood is one of the larger Forestry Commission holdings in Kent and there are plenty of tracks to explore. As there are no waymarked singletrack trails, this ride sticks to the broad forest roads where you are less likely to get lost. Chilham is a picture postcard village, complete with castle, square, fine old timbered buildings and a good pub and tearoom.

The Ride

Leave Chilham's picturesque square, soon joining the dead-end road of Mountain Street. Climb steeply at the end of tarmac on a broad track to the edge of King's Wood. A short rough and muddy patch at the top is the exception rather than the rule, as you descend to the A252, then climb once again off-road up to Shottenden. Quiet lanes through rich, arable land lead to the sneaky track that takes you into the fine and attractive woodland of King's Wood. A long blast of a downhill on forest road is followed by a short climb with ever better views out over the Stour Valley. The outward route is joined for bouncy bounce fun back to the tarmac and Chilham's watering holes.

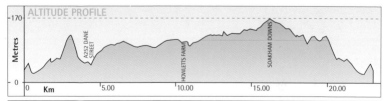

ALTITUDE PROFILE

A252 DANE STREET — HOWLETTS FARM — SOAKHAM DOWNS

Metres: 0 – 170

Km: 0 — 5.00 — 10.00 — 15.00 — 20.00

CHILHAM & KING'S WOOD

GRADE: ▲

DISTANCE: 23KM

TOTAL ASCENT: 240M

START/FINISH: CHILHAM, OFF THE A28 BETWEEN ASHFORD & CANTERBURY   **GRID REFERENCE:** GR 066 536

PARKING: LARGE FREE CAR PARK IN CHILHAM AT GR 066 536   **CAFÉ:** COPPER KETTLE TEA ROOMS, CHILHAM Tel: 01227 730 303

PUBLIC HOUSE: WHITE HORSE, CHILHAM Tel: 01227 730 355

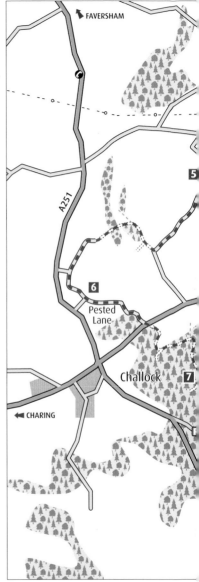

Chilham & King's Wood

Directions — Chilham & King's Wood

⊙➤ Exit the main car park in Chilham and turn **R**. In the square, turn **R** onto School Hill, then shortly, at a T-junction, turn **R** again onto Mountain Street. After 2km, at the end of the tarmac, as the main track swings sharp left, bear **R** (in effect **SA**) through a gate onto a wide stone track alongside trees.

2 Follow the main track as it swings **R**. Steady climb. At the top go **SA** onto a rutted track, ignoring a left turn through a metal gate. (This is the return route.) The first 400m are muddy after rain.

3 Descend and join tarmac. At the T-junction with the A252 at the end of Dane Street, turn **L** along the pavement. Shortly after the end of the trees/hedge to the right, turn sharp **R** on a broad stone track signposted *Byway*.

4 Climb steadily. Join tarmac. At the T-junction (where power lines cross the road) turn **R**. At the X-roads, turn **L** signposted *Molash, Charing*.

5 **Easy to miss**: after almost 2km, take the second road to the **L**, signposted *Challock, Ashford*. After a further 1.8km, as the road swings sharp left by a triangle of grass, turn **R**, signposted *Howletts, Byway*.

6 At the T-junction, by a large triangle of grass, turn **L**. At the T-junction with the A252 at the end of Pested Lane, turn **L** then **R** onto a narrow track leading into the woodland (no sign). Fine beech woods. At the T-junction with a broad forest road, turn **L**.

7 After almost 1km, at a major track junction with cypress trees to your left, **ignore** a left turn then a right turn, following the main track towards the wooden gateposts.

8 **Ignore** several earth tracks to right and left. At the next T-junction with coppiced sweet chestnut ahead, turn **R** to continue gently uphill and then shortly turn sharp **L**.

9 Long, easy descent. Start to climb. At a junction of tracks after an earth 'chicane', bear **L**, joining the North Downs Way. Great views to the right. Rejoin the outward route by a metal gate and a wooden bridlegate. Turn **R** for fine descent.

10 Join tarmac. After almost 2km, on a sharp **RH** bend, turn **L** up School Hill, then **L** again at the end of the square in Chilham to return to the car park.

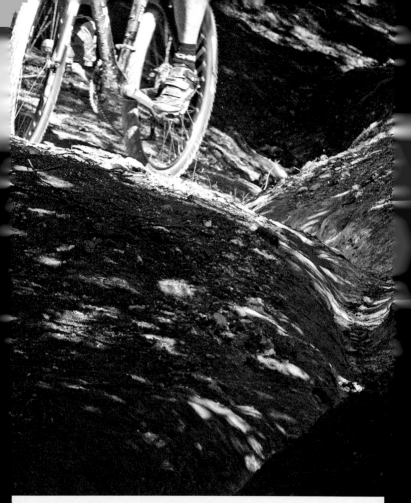

◀◌⊙◌ Making a day of it

A short section of the busy A28 northeast of Chilham through Bagham connects to a minor lane that in turn links with the **Shalmsford Street** ride *(see page 71)* at **GR 092 539**. The Forestry Commission owns King's Wood, so there are plenty of tracks to explore in the woodlands. There are some fine tracks on the Crundale Downs to the east of Wye. Another easy ride follows the North Downs Way west from Charing Hill (northwest of Ashford) on a mixture of byways and minor lanes to the pub in Hollingbourne.

10 Shalmsford Street & Chartham Downs

21km

Introduction

This was going to be a much longer ride, but many of Kent's bridleways seem to be popular with horses and horse-hoof damage makes many tracks all but unrideable. This shortened version picks out the best of the rest, offering a fine little ride within easy striking distance of Canterbury. The ride has a predominantly wooded feel to it – the southern half of Denge Wood and Eggringe Wood are owned by the Forestry Commission and offer scope for designing your own singletrack routes.

The Ride

Zoom downhill on tarmac along Mystole Lane to the start of a long off-road climb through woodland with an exit out into open pasture that is easily missed. If your nose starts twitching it's probably the glue factory in the heart of Eggringe Wood, a powerful stench on a bad day! The Compasses Inn at Sole Street is your only chance of refreshment on the route and comes at the southern-most point. Head north on a fine broad track that feels like an old road fallen into disuse. The final off-road section in Larkeyvalley Wood provides the best descent of the day before you turn south once again for Shalmsford Street.

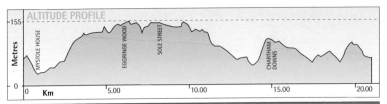

SHALMSFORD STREET & CHARTHAM DOWNS   GRADE: ▲

DISTANCE: 21KM   **TOTAL ASCENT:** 290M

START/FINISH: EAST END OF SHALMSFORD ST, OFF THE A28, SOUTHWEST OF CANTERBURY   **GRID REFERENCE:** GR 108 544

PARKING: ROADSIDE VERGE AT THE EAST END OF SHALMSFORD ST. (GR 108 544)   **CAFÉ:** BRING SANDWICHES

PUBLIC HOUSE: COMPASSES, SOLE STREET Tel: 01227 700 300

Chilham

A28

ASHFORD

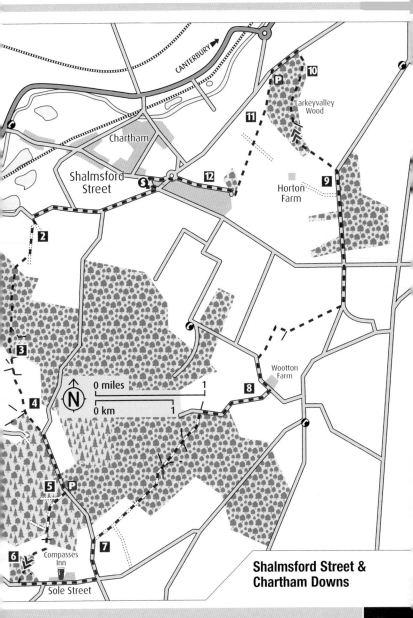

Directions – Shalmsford Street & Chartham Downs

➊ Climb east from the junction of Shalmsford Street and The Crescent (GR 108 544). After 200m turn **R** at X-roads onto Mystole Lane signposted *Mystole*. Fast descent, gentle climb.

2 After 1.5km, as the road swings sharp right downhill (Pickleden Lane), turn **L**, signposted *Private, no through road*. Shortly, turn first **R** onto a broad gravel track towards Barnyard Stables, waymarked with a low stone *Bridleway* sign. Go past the stables and follow a broad track across a field.

3 Enter woodland, take the **LH** track and climb steadily on a good earth and stone track. Parts will be muddy after rain. Stay on the broad track. **Easy to miss**: after 1km, keep an eye out for a square wooden post on your right, with blue and yellow arrows. About 100m after this post, as the track swings sharp right, bear **L** onto a narrower track to go into the field via a bridlegate (GR 089 523).

4 **Easy to miss**: after 300m, at a fork of grassy tracks, as the **LH** track follows the edge of the woodland, bear **R** towards a small lonesome tree and post. At a X-roads with a footpath by the post go **SA**. Go through a bridlegate and across another field. Go through another bridlegate into woodland.

5 At the T-junction with the road, turn **R**. After 800m, opposite a car parking area to the left, turn **R** onto a smooth gravel track. Shortly at a fork, bear **L** – there is a metal barrier to the right. Emerge from the woodland, following a track with fields to either side.

6 Re-enter woodland and you come to a junction of several tracks – the first two lead to fields on the right. Take the woodland track leading downhill to the **R**. At the road, turn **L**, climb steeply, go past the Compasses Inn at Sole Street.

7 At the X-roads of lanes, turn **L** signposted *Chartham*. After 500m, take the first broad stone track between hedges to the **R**, signposted *Bridleway*. Fine easy track that used to be road runs through woodland.

8 At the T-junction with a minor lane in the wood, turn **R**. At the T-junction at the end of Capel Lane, opposite Wootton Barn, turn **L**. **Easy to miss**: on a gentle **LH** bend at the bottom of a dip, shortly after a small red-brick water pumping house on your right, turn **R** on a narrow woodland track, signposted *Bridleway* (this comes just before the *End of Speed Limit* signs).

9 Generally downhill. Emerge at the road and turn **L**. Climb. At the X-roads with a busy road, go **SA** to continue climbing. About 200m after passing a tarmac drive to Horton Farm to the left, keep an eye out for a *Bridleway* sign to the **L**, onto a broad earth track along the field edge where the woodland starts on the left.

10 Enter woodland and at the first fork of tracks, after 300m, turn **R** downhill. **Ignore** turns to right and left. Emerge at the road by a Larkeyvalley Wood information board. Turn **L** uphill.

11 After 450m, at the brow of the hill, turn **L** through car park onto a broad stone track to continue uphill. At the top of the climb, bear **R** off the main track onto a narrower earth track alongside the fence.

12 Descend, then climb on singletrack, at times very narrow. At the top of the climb, opposite a children's play area to the left, turn **R** through a new housing estate. Ignore a left turn on Chestnut Close. Continue **SA**. At the roundabout at the end of Beech Avenue, turn **L**, signposted *Chartham*, then bear **R** onto The Crescent to return to the start.

◀️⚙️ Making a day of it

Chilham *(see page 65)* lies only a short distance southwest of Shalmsford Street. There are lots of good quality tracks on the Crundale Downs just east of the village of Wye (south of this ride).

SECTION 2

South Downs

Big skies, big views of the English Channel and the Sussex Weald, granny ring climbs and swooping chalk and flint descents, huge fields of corn rippling in the breeze, fringed with bright red poppies, skylarks hovering above, woodland floors carpeted with bluebells in the spring... Rides along the South Downs offer a sense of space that you don't expect to find in the crowded South East.

South Downs
sponsored by

www.bikemagic.com

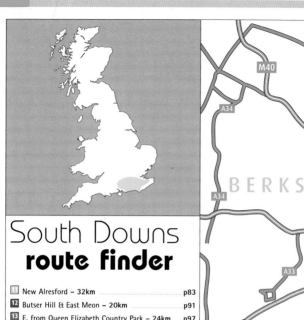

South Downs
route finder

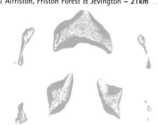

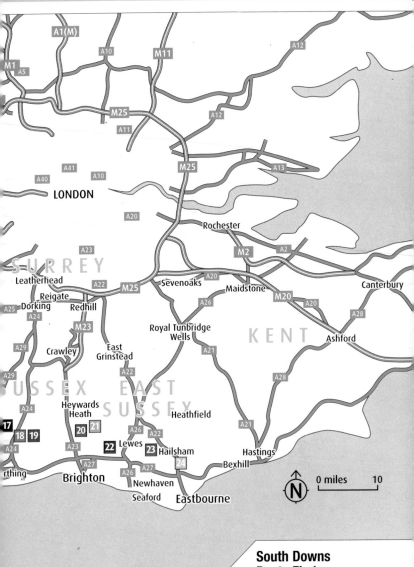

**South Downs
Route Finder**

11 New Alresford

Introduction

The start of the South Downs Way, between Winchester and the Meon Valley, has a much gentler feel than the more dramatic hills that lie further east. This ride is a quiet celebration of the English countryside, a gentle unfolding, with no sharp edges. It's a good ride to do after a few dry days in mid-summer or through into autumn with the changing colours. A ride to be avoided in winter and after prolonged rain as the low-lying terrain can get sticky...

The Ride

Leave the handsome town of New Alresford, cross the bridge over the A31 and dive into the network of tracks and tiny lanes that runs southwest through Tichborne to Gander Down to join the South Downs Way. This is followed on track and lane past the Milbury's pub to the highpoint of the ride near the nature reserve on Beacon Hill. Having climbed this high (190m/625ft) you won't be surprised that you now have the best views and the best descent of the day. 4x4s have wrecked many of the tracks north of Warnford, hence more lanes than off-road until you are through Hinton Ampner and back onto broad chalk and flint tracks leading right to the edge of New Alresford.

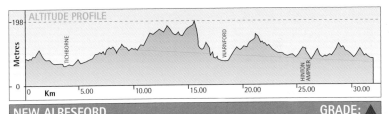

ALTITUDE PROFILE

198 — Metres — 0

TICHBORNE · WARNFORD · HINTON AMPNER

Km 5.00 10.00 15.00 20.00 25.00 30.00

NEW ALRESFORD GRADE: ▲

DISTANCE: 32KM

START/FINISH: NEW ALRESFORD

TOTAL ASCENT: 250M

GRID REFERENCE: GR 589 325

PARKING: FOLLOW SIGNS FOR 'WATERCRESS LINE' FROM THE CENTRE OF TOWN ALONG STATION ROAD (GR 589 325).

CAFÉ: LOTS OF CHOICE IN NEW ALRESFORD. **PUBLIC HOUSE:** LOTS OF CHOICE IN NEW ALRESFORD.

TICHBORNE ARMS, TICHBORNE. MILBURY'S, SOUTH OF BEAUWORTH. GEORGE & FALCON, WARNFORD.

New Alresford

Directions – New Alresford

➎ From the main car park by the Watercress Line railway station, follow signs for *Overflow car park*. At the T-junction, with the Methodist church ahead, turn **L** under the railway bridge. Climb then descend. Go past the Cricketers pub, cross the bridge over the A31. **Easy to miss**: immediately after the end of the bridge railings, turn **R** onto a narrow stone and gravel track alongside the main road.

2 Follow the track as it swings **L** away from the A31 and becomes an earth and stone track, at times overgrown. Join a wide gravel track by a brick house on the right. At the T-junction with the road, turn **L**. Go past the Tichborne Arms pub. About 300m after the pub, on the **second** sharp **LH** bend, with a large wooden barn ahead, turn **R** onto a broad stone track to go past Grange Farm, signposted *Bridleway*.

3 Follow this track for 2.5km, eventually heading for a barn on the horizon (it has a pylon behind it). At the junction of tracks at the barn, turn **L** signposted *South Downs Way*. Descend to pass beneath the power lines and take the **LH** grassy track at the fork – **not** towards the barn, in other words.

4 Go through a bridlegate and stay on the main track on the left-hand edge of the field. At the corner of the field, before a metal gate that leads into woodland, turn sharp **R** on a broad grass track, keeping the hedge to your left. Shortly, at a 3-way signpost, turn **L** downhill on a broad chalk track, signposted *South Downs Way*.

5 At a X-roads with the busy A272, go **SA** towards Holden Farm, signposted *South Downs Way*. At a X-roads of tracks continue **SA** (same sign). After 500m, at the T-junction with a road by a barn, bear **R** (in effect **SA**) gently uphill, signposted *South Downs Way*. At a T-junction by a triangle of grass, turn **R** uphill, then take the first road to the **L** after Milbury's pub, signposted *Warnford*.

6 The South Downs Way soon diverts off the road onto a parallel track to the left. After 1.3km, where this ends, cross the road onto a broad stone track through a metal gate, signposted *Wind Farm*. Shortly, as the main track swings right to follow the telegraph poles, bear **L** alongside a neat garden hedge on a grass and chalk track, signposted *South Downs Way*.

7 Keep following the South Downs Way on the main track as it swings left between houses and barns. Shortly after the start of tarmac and after the last barn on the right, turn **R** onto a broad stone track signposted *South Downs Way*. At the road, bear **L** – in effect **SA**. Views opening up to the right. After 200m, on a **RH** bend, turn sharp **L** through a car parking area, signposted *South Downs Way*.

8 Exit woodland onto a narrow track across a field, parallel to a private road down to the right. After almost 1.5km, at a T-junction with a broad stone track with a *Private* sign ahead, turn **R** through a metal gate and then **L** downhill. At the T-junction with the road by the Wheely Down Forge, turn **R**. At the T-junction with the busy A32, turn **L** – use South Downs Way along pavement. Shortly, turn **L** again on Lippen Lane – or go **SA** for the George & Falcon pub.

9 Climb gently on tarmac for 2km. At the T-junction at the end of Lippen Lane, turn **L**, signposted *Bramdean*. Climb for a further 300m, then bear **L** onto a brown gravel track and immediately **L** again onto an earth track between hedgerows. Muddy after rain. At the T-junction with the road, turn **L**. At the fork of lanes after 500m, bear **R** signposted *Cheriton*.

10 After almost 2km, at a lane junction near two red-brick houses, go **SA** onto an improved track (blue arrow). At the T-junction with the next road, with an avenue of trees to your left and a rutted mud track ahead, turn **R** gently uphill.

11 Go through the village of Hinton Ampner, descend to the A272 and go **SA** onto a no through road, signposted *Wayfarer's Walk*. Climb on a broad chalk and flint track. At a X-roads with a similar track by a height barrier, beneath power lines, continue **SA** uphill.

12 Descend from the brow. At the road turn **R**. Climb, go round two **LH** bends then on a **RH** bend, bear **L** – in effect **SA** – to continue uphill on a chalk and flint track towards the mast. At a fork of tracks, bear **L**. At the T-junction near water treatment works, turn **L** then **R** onto a narrow path.

DIRECTIONS CONTINUE ON NEXT PAGE

Directions – New Alresford
Continued

13   At the 7th tee of the golf course, turn **R** then **L**, signposted *Bridleway*. At the T-junction of trails at the end of the golf course, with the A31 ahead, turn **L**. Cross the footbridge over the main road, bear **R** at the end of the bridge, then **R** again with the road.

14   At the T-junction at the end of Sun Lane, turn **L** into New Alresford. After 500m turn **L** again on Station Road, signposted *Watercress Line*, to return to the car park at the start.

◄ Making a day of it

The best link to the **East Meon** ride *(page 91)* would be via the lane along the Meon Valley between West Meon and East Meon. Other rides to the north of the A31 can be found in our second volume to the area – **South East Mountain Biking – Chilterns & Ridgeway**.

12 Butser Hill & East Meon

20km

Introduction

At 270m/885ft, Butser Hill is the highest point along the course of the South Downs Way. Your first view of the ascent from the west side of the A3 is of a huge grass slope leading to the mast – a good challenge to climb without a dab and a very fine descent at the end of the ride. Talking of downhills, the descent from Butser Hill to the north is about as close as it gets to technical in the South Downs, although the tougher right-hand option looks in danger of becoming an eroded narrow gully. The ride also enjoys two good pubs in the picturesque village of East Meon and a long challenging climb up past the masts on Wether Down.

The Ride

No chance of a warm-up; you are soon faced with the long climb to the top of Butser Hill and a choice of steep chalky descents down into the Meon Valley. There is a wet weather/mud warning on the next off-road section – use the lane alternative if there's been a lot of recent rain. East Meon and its church are quintessential England. A short lane section down the valley precedes a long off-road climb through stunning woodland, then an ever-steeper challenge up to the plateau by the mast. The South Downs Way is followed on easy tracks back to Butser Hill for that final grassy whooooosh!

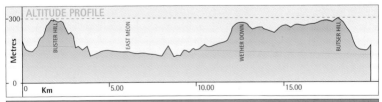

ALTITUDE PROFILE

BUTSER HILL

EAST MEON

WETHER DOWN

BUTSER HILL

Metres

300

0

| 0 | Km | 5.00 | 10.00 | 15.00 |

BUTSER HILL & EAST MEON

GRADE: ▲

DISTANCE: 20KM

TOTAL ASCENT: 370M

START/FINISH: QUEEN ELIZABETH COUNTRY PARK, JUST OFF THE A3, ABOUT 4 MILES SOUTH OF PETERSFIELD

GRID REFERENCE: GR 720 184

PARKING: PAY & DISPLAY CAR PARK (GR 720 184)

CAFÉ: AT THE Q.E.C.P VISITOR CENTRE Tel: 023 9259 5040

PUBLIC HOUSE: ISAAK WALTON, EAST MEON Tel: 01730

823 252 or OLD GEORGE INN, EAST MEON Tel: 01730 823 481

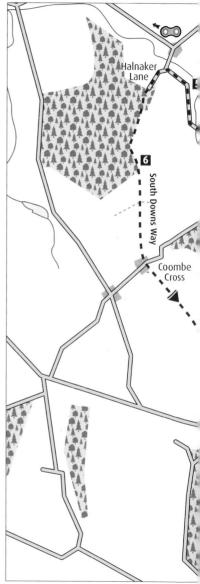

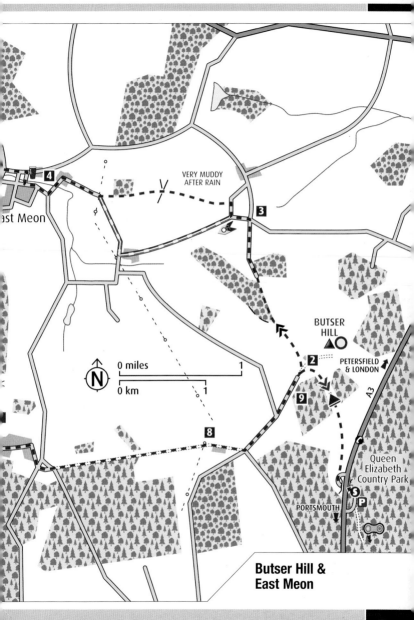

VERY MUDDY
AFTER RAIN

East Meon

4

3

BUTSER
HILL

2

PETERSFIELD
& LONDON

9

A3

0 miles · · · · · 1

0 km · · · · · 1

N

8

Queen
Elizabeth
Country Park

5

P

PORTSMOUTH

Butser Hill &
East Meon

Directions – Butser Hill & East Meon

1 Exit the Queen Elizabeth Country Park car park back towards the A3. Turn **R**, signposted *Petersfield*, pass beneath the A3, then turn **L** onto a tarmac path, signposted *South Downs Way*. Aim towards the tall, blue-tipped wooden posts along the light brown gravel path. Challenging grassy climb beyond first bridlegate.

2 Go through a second bridlegate and aim towards a pyramid-shaped building. Go through a third bridlegate and bear **L**. Join tarmac, turn **L**, cross the speed humps. At the next metal barrier, turn sharp **R**, signposted *No cars* (red & white road sign). After 700m at a fork of tracks, bear **R*** alongside the fence for a technical descent, followed by an undulating wide track of variable surface quality.

    *The left-hand fork is also a good descent: less technical but with better surface quality. If you choose this, turn **R** at the road at the bottom, then **L**, rejoining at the next instruction *"Shortly take the first wide stone track..."*

3 At a X-roads with the road at the bottom, turn **L**. After 400m, take the first lane **R*** (no sign). Shortly take the first wide stone track to the **L**, signposted *No cars*. At an offset X-roads of grassy tracks, turn **R** then **L** to continue in the same direction. The rough and rutted track becomes a wide gravel 'drive'. At the road, bear **R**.

    *A rough 800m section in the middle of this off-road stretch will be muddy after rain. For a lane alternative, continue **SA** on the minor lane for 1.3km, then on a sharp **LH** bend, take the first road **R** by a triangle of grass, signposted *Frogmore* into East Meon, rejoining at the start of next instruction.

4 At the T-junction by the blacksmith's forge, turn **R**. Go through the village of East Meon, past the Isaak Walton pub and follow the road as it swings right past the Old George Inn. At the T-junction, with the church ahead, turn **L**.

5 Follow signs for *West Meon*. After 1.5km, on the **second** sharp **RH** bend, turn **L** sharply uphill onto Halnaker Lane, signposted *Byway*. Shortly, fork **L** onto a wide stone track. At a metal and wood barrier, keep **L** on the lower earth and stone track.

6 Tracks run parallel – take either and continue in the same direction. After 1.3km the South Downs Way joins from the right. After a further 750m, at a X-roads with a lane by a house called Coombe Cross, continue **SA**, signposted *South Downs Way*, onto a broad gravel track.

7 Steep 1.5km climb on chalk, with occasional roots, potentially slippery. Go past the masts then at the road, turn **L** alongside a barbed wire compound. After 1km at the T-junction, by a *Give Way* sign, continue **SA** onto the track opposite, signposted *South Downs Way, Unsuitable for HGVs*.

8 Fine track. Go past the farm. At the road junction, turn **L** then **L** again onto Hogs Lodge Lane, signposted *Butser Hill picnic area*. After 1km, at the brown and white *Queen Elizabeth Country Park/Butser Hill* signpost, bear **R** onto an earth track, signposted *South Downs Way*. This rejoins the outward route.

9 Go through a bridlegate and bear **R**, contouring across the short grass. Go through the next bridlegate and enjoy the wide grassy descent. Follow blue arrows back under the A3 to return to the visitor centre.

◄⃝⃝ Making a day of it

Another ride heads **East from Queen Elizabeth Country Park** *(see page 97)*. The **New Alresford** ride *(page 83)* could be joined by following the lane along the valley from East Meon to West Meon.

13 East from Queen Elizabeth Country Park

24km

Introduction

Queen Elizabeth Country Park is a popular base for mountain biking; located close to the A3, there are fine tracks west up onto Butser Hill, a couple of easy waymarked trails in the surrounding Forestry Commission woodland and a good café at the visitor centre where you can fuel up before or after the rides. The South Downs Way forms the northern half of this ride, with the pattern set for many of the rides further east: a steep climb up onto the ridge, with fantastic views out over the Sussex Weald and long, easy ridge sections on broad chalk and grass tracks.

The Ride

Starting parallel with the A3, the track soon veers away from the road and the noise fades as you follow the narrow stone-based track towards the village of Chalton. One of those timeless old unsurfaced coach roads through broadleaf woodland takes you east, briefly joining the lane network before dropping down into the unusual dry grassy valley below Harting Downs. A steep grassy climb takes you up to the South Downs Way and the best views of the day, looking down across the villages in the Weald. Follow the South Downs Way up and down through woodland and farmland back to Queen Elizabeth Country Park.

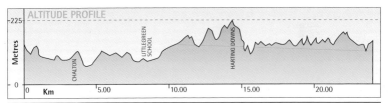

ALTITUDE PROFILE

225 — Metres — 0

CHALTON — LITTLEGREEN SCHOOL — HARTING DOWNS

Km — 0 — 5.00 — 10.00 — 15.00 — 20.00

EAST FROM QUEEN ELIZABETH COUNTRY PARK — **GRADE:** ▲

DISTANCE: 24KM

TOTAL ASCENT: 390M

START/FINISH: QUEEN ELIZABETH COUNTRY PARK, OFF THE A3

GRID REFERENCE: GR 720 184

PARKING: PAY & DISPLAY CAR PARK (GR 720 184)

CAFÉ: AT THE Q.E.C.P VISITOR CENTRE Tel: 023 9259 5040

PUBLIC HOUSE: RED LION, CHALTON Tel: 023 9259 2246. COACH & HORSES, COMPTON Tel: 023 9263 1228

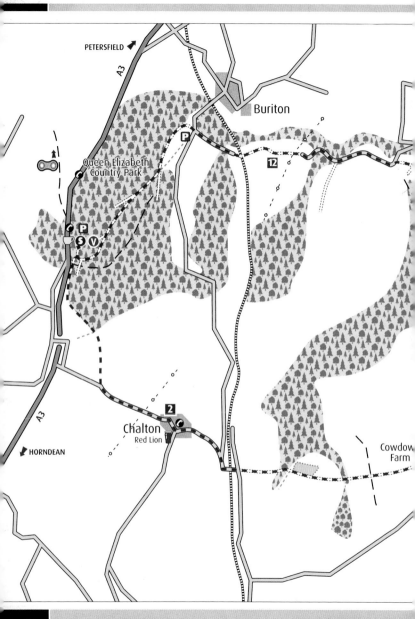

PETERSFIELD

A3

Buriton

Queen Elizabeth
Country Park

P

12

S V

2

Chalton
Red Lion

A3

HORNDEAN

Cowdown
Farm

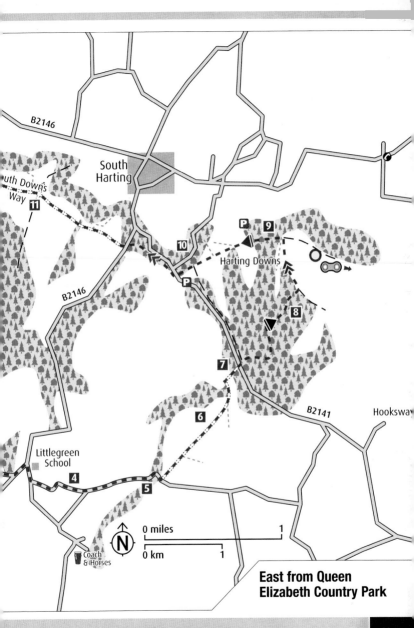

**East from Queen
Elizabeth Country Park**

Directions — East from Queen Elizabeth Country Park

↪ From the Queen Elizabeth Country Park car park, follow signs for *Bikes/Horseboxes* on the tarmac lane alongside the visitor centre. On a sharp **LH** bend, shortly before a Pay & Display machine, turn **R** towards a blue-topped marker, signposted *No Unauthorised Vehicles*. Keep bearing **R**, following the white bike/blue arrow waymarks. Follow the narrow stone-based track, at first parallel to the A3.

2 At the T-junction with the lane, turn **L** and go into Chalton. At the triangle of grass just before the telephone box and the Red Lion pub, turn **L**, signposted *Ditcham*. Climb, then fast descent. At a road T-junction, 100m after crossing the railway bridge, go **SA** onto a broad stone track (no sign).

3 Follow this track for 3km, climbing and descending. Go through Cowdown Farm as the track turns to concrete then tarmac. At the T-junction with the lane by black metal lamplights, turn **L**.

4 At the T-junction with the B2146 by Littlegreen School, turn **R**, signposted *Compton*, then shortly **L**, signposted *6 ft 6 ins width limit*. At the next T-junction of lanes by One Hundred Acres Farm, bear **L**.

5 Climb on tarmac for 1.2km. At a X-roads of tracks in a clearing near the top of the hill, with a 3-way *Bridleway* signpost on the **RH** side of the road, turn **L** onto a broad chalk and stone track.

6 Follow this track in the same direction along the **RH** field edge as it narrows to earth singletrack. Go through a wide metal gate, following the line of telegraph poles. At the end of the fenced field to the left, bear **R** through a gap onto a track continuing in the same direction.

7 Join a wider track by a house on the right. Just before the road, turn **L** onto a parallel track. Cross the B2141 onto the bridleway opposite. Shortly, fork **R** to join a wider track, following the blue arrow.

8 The track swings left steeply downhill into a dry valley. At a wooden post with blue and yellow arrows, turn **R** steeply uphill. At the T-junction with the South Downs Way at the top of the climb, turn **L** downhill. You are following the South Downs Way all the way back to Queen Elizabeth Country Park.

9 After a fast descent, you come to a X-roads of tracks in a large grassy clearing with a tall wooden post on a round flint base. Turn **L** uphill, signposted *Buriton, South Downs Way* – **not** the gated track to the left.

10 Climb to highpoint. Descend, keeping **R** to go through a bridlegate. Then bear **R** away from the car parking area. Aim across a grassy clearing towards a wooden signpost and narrow track/gap, through woodland to the road. Cross the road (B2141) with care onto bridleway opposite. Fast descent. At the next road (B2146), cross, once again with care, onto bridleway opposite.

11 At X-roads with tarmac, by a house and a low red-brick barn, go **SA**. Climb then descend. At T-junction with tarmac, turn **L**, signposted *South Downs Way*. After 800m take the first lane to the **R**, by a triangle of grass.

12 Follow the tarmac as it turns to track and passes beneath power lines. Several ups and downs. The track becomes tarmac again. At X-roads, go **SA** through Halls Hill car park and onto the track ahead. Climb steeply. At the track junction at the brow of the hill, bear **L**. Shortly, fork **R** on the lower track, signposted *South Downs Way, Walkers & Cyclists*. At the tarmac, bear **L** to return to the car park and visitor centre.

◄◉⊃ **Making a day of it**

Another ride heads west from the visitor centre up onto **Butser Hill** *(see page 91)*. To the east you can link via a 3km section of the South Downs Way to the **Goodwood & Hooksway** ride *(see page 103)*.

14 Goodwood & Hooksway

31km

Introduction

Combining views out to sea with views over the Sussex Weald, this ride gives a real flavour of the variety of mountain biking in the area. Throw in a chance to race against the gee gees at Goodwood (the bridleway runs parallel to the racecourse), good pubs at Charlton and Hooksway, a couple of 'throw down the gauntlet' climbs and a cracking descent to finish and you have a South Downs classic.

The Ride

There are four major climbs on this ride and it starts as it means to go on, with a 130m ascent along the South Downs Way, east from the A286. This sets you up for a fast, narrow and at times overgrown descent through the forest, eventually spitting you out in the pretty village of Charlton. Climb past Goodwood racecourse, soon rewarded with great views out to Chichester Harbour. Descents and climbs follow in dizzying succession. Your final chance of a bracer comes at the Royal Oak at Hooksway, before the final climb and a magnificent 5km of cruising. Then it's downhill back to the start.

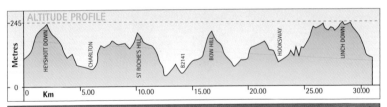

DISTANCE: 31KM	TOTAL ASCENT: 750M
START/FINISH: COCKING HILL CAR PARK ON THE A286 BETWEEN MIDHURST AND CHICHESTER	
GRID REFERENCE: GR 876 167	PARKING: AS OPPOSITE AT GR 876 167
CAFÉ: BRING SANDWICHES	PUBLIC HOUSE: FOX GOES FREE, CHARLTON Tel: 01243

GOODWOOD & HOOKSWAY   **GRADE:** ▲

811 461. ROYAL OAK, HOOKSWAY Tel: 01243 535 257

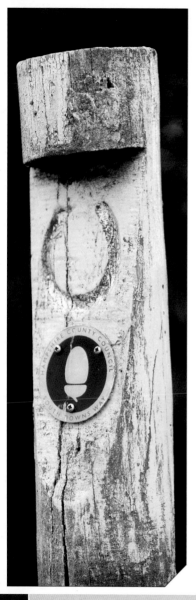

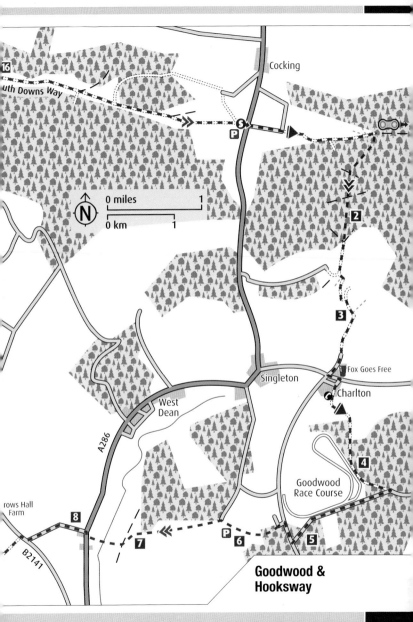

Cocking

South Downs Way

16

0 miles 1
0 km 1

N

S
P

2

3

Fox Goes Free

Singleton

Charlton

West
Dean

A286

4

Goodwood
Race Course

rows Hall
Farm

8

B2141

7

P
6

5

**Goodwood &
Hooksway**

Directions – Goodwood & Hooksway

❸ From the Cocking Hill car park, cross the A286 onto the no through road on the opposite side, heading east. Climb for 1.5km. **Ignore** the first right turn at the start of woodland. Go past a 4-way signpost with yellow arrows (footpaths) to right and left. After 150m, at the next 4-way signpost (green and blue arrows) and at the end of a small clump of trees to the left, turn **R** onto a grassy track.

2 Continue **SA** downhill on this narrow (and at times overgrown) track for 1.5km, across a series of X-roads. As the gradient levels out and the track becomes more earth and less stone, at a fork of tracks by a wooden post with two blue arrows and with a field to the right, bear **L**. After 400m, at a major junction of tracks with several signposts and a *Drovers Estate National Trust* sign, bear **L** downhill on a broad track.

3 Fast descent. At a T-junction, with a small wooden stile in the fence ahead, turn **R** to continue downhill on a broad stone track. At the X-roads in Charlton, at the end of North Lane, turn **L** past flint houses. Turn **R** opposite the Fox Goes Free pub, signposted *Unsuitable for HGVs*, and head towards a telephone box. The lane swings right, then immediately left. Follow *Bridleway* signs as the tarmac turns to track.

4 Climb on a broad chalk and flint track. At the junction at the top of the climb, bear **L** to continue uphill. Goodwood racecourse is to the right. At the T-junction with the road, turn **R** (this will be busy during race meetings).

5 After 1.5km, at the T-junction, turn **R**, signposted *Singleton, Midhurst*. After 350m, turn **L** onto a tarmac access road with metal barriers, signposted *Owners & Trainers only, Bridleway*. **Easy to miss**: shortly, at the end of low wooden car park fence on the left, turn **L** off tarmac onto a narrow track signposted *Bridleway* (the sign may be hidden by a tree).

6 Climb steeply then more gently through woodland. Suddenly you are out in the open with sea views. Cross this grassy expanse and go past the car park. Cross the lane and take the **LH** (narrower) of the two tracks ahead, to the left of the low wooden posts. With an ornate flint and brick house to the right (The Rubbing House), bear **L** at a fork of tracks by a 3-way *bridleway* signpost.

7 Fast descent along a field edge. Go through a gate at the end of a small patch of woodland. Head diagonally **L** downhill across the next field, to another gate, aiming for the brick and flint houses ahead. Join the Centurion Way, a railway path linking Chichester to West Dean, and continue **SA**.

8 At the T-junction with the busy A286, turn **R** then **L** up Binderton Lane. Climb to the brow and follow the lane downhill around a left-hand bend, **ignoring** the bridleway ahead. At the T-junction with the B2141, turn **R** then immediately **L**, signposted *Keep to bridlepaths*. Go through a metal field gate about 50m before a farm.

9 **Easy to miss**: after 1.5km, you come to the top of a gentle climb. At the end of the hedgerow/line of trees on the left, there is a X-roads of tracks marked by a wooden post with blue arrows. Turn **R** uphill, between wire fences, heading towards the round wooded hill. Steady climb, with the gradient steepening after the first *Kingley Vale* signboard. At a X-roads of tracks by a second *Kingley Vale* information board and a 4-way *Bridleway* signpost, continue **SA** uphill.

10 Continue climbing briefly then descend, with one short, very dark section through conifers. Keep heading downhill. Shortly, at a mega-junction of tracks, continue **SA** downhill on the steeper of two tracks. At the bottom of a fast section, bear **L** to continue downhill on a wide gravel forest road.

11 **Easy to miss**: at the lowest point, just before the track starts to climb again, turn **R** sharply back on yourself. This wide grassy track is just before a 3-way *Bridleway* signpost (GR 818 129). The first section will be muddy after wet weather. Grass turns to gravel after 800m. Go past a serpent-like line of smooth-limbed beech trees then yew trees.

12 At the top of a long climb, you reach a junction with a more defined track. At a gap in the trees to the left, turn **L** through a bridlegate marked with a blue arrow. Enter a field and onto a rough grass track. Aim towards, then alongside, a copse of broadleaf trees, which eventually heads towards the barn and red-brick farm on the horizon. Great open views.

DIRECTIONS CONTINUE ON NEXT PAGE

Directions – Goodwood & Hooksway
Continued

13 Join the farm drive then a concrete track through the farm, following *Bridleway* signs. At the T-junction with the lane at the bottom of the drive, turn **R** then shortly **R*** again at the T-junction with the B2141, signposted *Chilgrove.*

*After prolonged rain it is worth avoiding the next, potentially muddy, off-road section. For a road alternative, turn **L** on the busy B2141 for almost 2km, then take the first road to the **R** signposted *'Hooksway'*. Rejoin at Instruction 15: *'At the fork of tracks beyond the pub...'*

14 **Very easy to miss!** Do not pick up terminal velocity on this fast downhill. After 450m, turn sharp **L** back on yourself onto a track signposted *West Dean Estate, bridleway only.* The lowest section will be muddy after prolonged rain. After almost 600m on this track, bear **L** at a fork on the lower track, signposted *West Dean Estate, bridleway only.*

15 Parts of this track are rutted by forestry vehicles. After 1km, at a T-junction with a lane, opposite the Royal Oak pub in Hooksway, turn **R**. At the fork of tracks beyond the pub, bear **R** – **not** the footpath to the far right. Steady climb for 1.2 km. At a X-roads of tracks by a 4-way signpost with red, blue and yellow arrows, continue **SA**.

16 Follow for almost 5km. Superb views out to sea and over the Sussex Weald. Join tarmac for a very fast descent to the Cocking Hill car park on the A286 at the start.

◄⊙⊙ **Making a day of it**

To the west, you can link with the **East from Queen Elizabeth Country Park** ride *(see page 97)* by using a short section of the South Downs Way near Hooksway. To the east you can use the South Downs Way over Graffham Down to link to the **Duncton Down** ride *(see page 111)*.

15 Eartham Wood, Duncton Down & Bignor Hill

21km

Introduction

Less than a kilometre of this ride is on tarmac, making it one of the 'purest' off-road rides in the book. The only drawback is that this means it passes no cafés or pubs, so come prepared with supplies. There are some stunning downland views along the way – all soft green folds, draped with broadleaf woodland, and huge fields of grain or pasture. For downhill aficionados, just off this ride, there is a series of bridleways – at least eight between the A285 and the A286 – that drop steeply to the north, off the South Downs escarpment from Graffham Down. Best to leave these for a dry spell at the end of summer, as they are north-facing and drain the hills behind.

The Ride

Climb through Eartham Wood on the old Roman road of Stane Street, turning off this at the massive signpost at the 6-way junction deep amongst the trees. Emerge from the woodland near the summit for a fine, fast descent to cross the A285 and start climbing again to the second highest point on the South Downs. Drop down past the quarry to join a balcony path on the other side of the A285, beyond Duncton Down viewpoint. The masts on Bignor Hill draw you on, up and down through woodland and fields of corn. You've reached 245m, you drop to 60m, you do the sums.

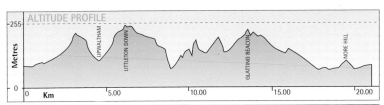

EARTHAM WOOD, DUNCTON DOWN & BIGNOR HILL   **GRADE:** ▲

DISTANCE: 21KM

START/FINISH: EARTHAM WOOD, 8 MILES SOUTH OF PETWORTH

PARKING: FORESTRY COMMISSION CAR PARK - GR 938 106. TURN OFF A285 AT SIGN FOR 'EARTHAM, SLINDON' THEN TURN 1ST LEFT

CAFÉ: BRING SANDWICHES

DOWN TO SUTTON OR NORTH ON THE A285 TOWARDS DUNCTON

TOTAL ASCENT: 500M

GRID REFERENCE: GR 938 106

PUBLIC HOUSE: NONE ON ROUTE. NEAREST IS A BIG DROP

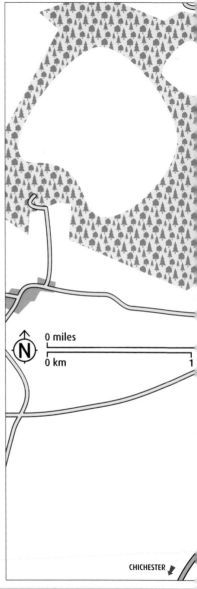

0 miles

N

0 km   1

CHICHESTER

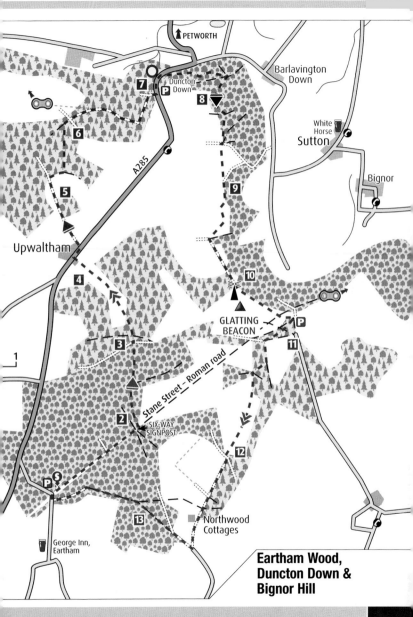

**Eartham Wood,
Duncton Down &
Bignor Hill**

PETWORTH

Barlavington
Down

White
Horse

Sutton

Bignor

Duncton
Down

A285

Upwaltham

Stane Street – Roman road

GLATTING
BEACON

SIX-WAY
SIGNPOST

Northwood
Cottages

George Inn,
Eartham

Directions – Eartham Wood, Duncton Down & Bignor Hill

➊ Exit the Eartham Wood car park back onto the road. Turn **L** then first **L** onto a broad forest track beyond a metal barrier. Shortly, at a fork of tracks by a 2-way *Bridleway* sign, bear **R** onto a chalk and flint track.

2 Climb gently, then the gradient steepens. After 1.5km, at a tall wooden 6-way *Stane Street* signpost, bear **L** to continue uphill. This track is signposted *Upwaltham* and goes to the right of the two posts with blue arrows.

3 Climb for 1.2km through mixed woodland. At the T-junction with a broad track, turn **R** then **L** (blue arrows) onto an earth and stone track. Continue **SA** at a 3-way signpost.

4 Exit woodland onto a wide, grass field-edge path. Cross between fields then start descending. At the bottom, there is a T-junction with tarmac, immediately before a flint farmhouse near the main road. Turn **R** onto a wide gravel track, keeping an eye out for a metal field gate and bridlegate to the **L**. This crosses the A285 onto the broad chalk and grass track that climbs the hill ahead and is signposted *Bridleway*.

5 Keep following *Bridleway* signs and blue arrows uphill as the chalk track turns to wide grassy track. At the corner of the field at the start of woodland, turn **R** (blue arrow) to continue uphill, with the wood now to your left.

6 At the top of the hill, turn **L** into woodland, signposted *Bridleway*, by two beech trees that stand clear of the wood. At the T-junction with a broader track, turn **R** signposted *Bridleway*. At the X-roads, go **SA**, signposted *Duncton*. Go down past the quarry, following *Right of Way* signs and red arrows.

7 At the T-junction with the A285, turn **L** downhill. After 250m, turn **L** again – keep your brakes on – into the viewpoint car park. Take stock of the traffic, then cross the busy A285 onto the track opposite. Follow this 'balcony' path.

8 At the 5-way track junction, turn **R** uphill, sharply back on yourself. After 200m, on a steady climb, turn **L** by a 3-way *Bridleway* sign onto a narrower track. A second 3-way sign follows shortly. Turn **R** very steeply uphill.

9 Climb to the edge of woodland and follow the narrow track with the field to the right. Superb views open up. Yes, you are heading for the mast on the horizon. Steep grassy descent then climb. At the end of the field continue in the same direction through a gate that opens onto a level track. The undulating track is, at times, narrow and overgrown.

10 At a T-junction with a wider track, by a 3-way *Bridleway* signpost, turn **R** uphill. At a fork of tracks just before the mast, bear **L** by a *National Trust, Bignor Hill* sign. Descend to the car parking area by a tall wooden signpost (this is behind a clump of bushes). Turn **R**, soon joining a wide chalk and flint track towards Slindon.

11 Shortly, at the X-roads of tracks, turn **R**, with the wood to your right and a field to your left. At the end of the field, turn **L** downhill, keeping woodland to your right. After 300m, turn first **R** into woodland by a wooden post with a blue arrow.

12 Long gentle descent, **ignoring** turns right and left. Pass to the **R** of a flint and brick barn. At a T-junction with a similar broad stone track, turn **L** to continue downhill. Go past Northwood Cottages and at the start of tarmac, turn **R** sharply back on yourself, by *National Trust Northwood and Bridleway* signs.

13 After 300m, bear **L** off the main track, through a bridlegate marked with a blue arrow, onto a narrow woodland path. Pass along a fenced field to your right, and re-enter woodland, climbing gently. At a X-roads of tracks by a signpost with blue arrows, turn **L** on a short steep climb. Continue **SA** at the top. Keep bearing **L** gently downhill then climb again. At the T-junction with the road, turn **R** then second **R** to return to the start.

◄◌◌ Making a day of it

Easily links to the west via a section of the South Downs Way to the **Goodwood & Hooksway** ride *(page 103)* and links directly with the **Slindon** ride on Bignor Hill. For the latter, it is best to start with the **Slindon** ride *(Instructions 1–8)* leaving at the 6-way signpost on Stane Street at **GR 952 114**. Do this ride then rejoin **Slindon** ride at **GR 951 104**.

16 Slindon & Bignor Hill

Introduction

The deluxe tea waggon known as the Hiker's Café in the car park by the roundabout at the junction of the A29 and A284 is an improbable destination, but it seems to draw you to its teas, coffees and cakes as though you have no choice in the matter. Perhaps because it's outdoors and it doesn't matter how muddy you are. From the 21st Century, travel back 2000 years; from the top of Bignor Hill you join Stane Street, an old Roman road that used to link London with Chichester. This is followed for several kilometres through pasture and woodland. And there is a jewel of a descent down to Slindon.

The Ride

Leave Slindon on a wide stone track, soon heading for the masts on the horizon. After crossing a vast sheep pasture you re-enter woodland and drop down fast on forest tracks and the Monarch's Way to the famous Hiker's Café. Tear yourself away from the bacon butties to join the South Downs Way as it climbs to the top of Bignor Hill. Straight as an arrow the old Roman road of Stane Street takes you past sheep and trees to the Eartham road. One final climb and you are set up for a fantastic gliding descent back down to Slindon.

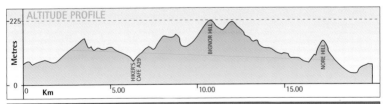

SLINDON & BIGNOR HILL **GRADE:** ▲

DISTANCE: 20KM **TOTAL ASCENT:** 350M

START/FINISH: SLINDON, NORTH OF THE A27 BETWEEN ARUNDEL AND CHICHESTER **GRID REFERENCE:** GR 961 084

PARKING: ON THE VERGE BY THE CHURCH IN SLINDON (GR 961 084) **CAFÉ:** HIKERS CAFÉ AT JUNCTION OF A29, A284 & B2139 WEST OF AMBERLEY

PUBLIC HOUSE: THE SPUR, SLINDON, ON THE A29 TO THE EAST OF THE VILLAGE Tel: 01243 814 216

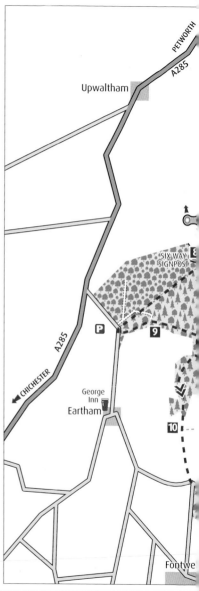

Upwaltham

PETWORTH

A285

SIX-WAY
SIGNPOST

CHICHESTER

A285

P

9

George
Inn

Eartham

10

Fontwe

Slindon & Bignor Hill

Directions – Slindon & Bignor Hill

➲ From the church in Slindon, follow the road north west towards Eartham. As the road swings left downhill, turn **R** opposite the entrance to Slindon College, through a field gate by a *National Trust* sign onto a wide stone bridleway.

2 After 800m, and immediately after passing a brick and flint barn with an enclosing wall on the left, bear **R** uphill. Continue towards the wooden posts and wire fence to join a narrow track between fields, signposted *Bridleroad* to Bignor. Long steady descent then long gentle climb, rough in parts. Exit the arable field via a bridlegate into pasture. Continue **SA** towards the wood on the horizon.

3 Go through the gate into the wood, then shortly turn **R** at a wooden post with a blue arrow. Cross the field and turn **R** then **L**, following bridleway signs downhill, continuing in the same direction on the track as it starts to climb.

4 At a X-roads of wide tracks in a clearing, go **SA**. Climb and follow the wide track with fields to either side. Go into woodland and follow blue arrows as the track swings **L**. Shortly, at a 3-way *Bridleway* sign, turn **R**. Fast downhill then follow *Monarch's Way* signs as it swings **R** and climbs. Descend to visit the Hiker's Café in the car park.

5 Retrace your steps from the Hiker's Café car park, back towards the wood via the wide red metal gate. **Easy to miss**: keep an eye out for the first narrow stone track uphill to the **R**, by a post with a blue arrow. Soon, at a T-junction, turn **L**. Follow the field edge uphill and round to the **R** (it may be overgrown). Steady climb. At the T-junction with the South Downs Way, bear **L** uphill.

6 Climb, flat section, downhill. After 1.7km, you come to the junction of tracks immediately beyond metal barns. Turn **L** to continue on the South Downs Way. At the T-junction at the top of a steep climb, turn **R**, signposted *South Downs Way*. Continue more gently uphill.

7 At the car park at the top, by a tall wooden signpost with Roman names, continue **SA** on the broad chalk and flint track. Climb between a *No cars* sign and the *Slindon Hill* information board. Bear immediately **L** on a grassy track along the edge of the woodland to your left. Stay on this main, wide, grassy track, soon descending through woodland as the surface turns to earth and grass.

8 At a X-roads of tracks by a 4-way signpost, go **SA** through a bridlegate to continue downhill. Follow the course of the old Roman road of Stane Street. Continue **SA** downhill at a mega track junction by a 6-way signpost and at several more X-roads of tracks. At the road, turn **L** then almost immediately **L** again onto a bridleway by a *Forestry Commission North Wood* sign.

9 At two forks of tracks, bear **R** each time (blue arrows). At a major X-roads of tracks, with a short wooden fence and a *No horses* sign to the left, turn **R** uphill (the track ahead starts to descend steeply beyond this point). Climb to the T-junction and turn **R** (blue arrow) to continue uphill.

10 Superb long descent. At T-junction with the road, turn **L** and follow back to the start in Slindon.

←◎ Making a day of it

The **Eartham Wood & Duncton Down** ride also climbs to the top of Bignor Hill. For the best link see *page 115*. To the east, a 4km section of the South Downs Way links this ride to the **Storrington** ride *(page 123)* at GR 038 125, south of Amberley.

17 Storrington & Kithurst Hill

28km

Introduction

Good quality singletrack in the South Downs is at a bit of a premium – most of the good riding is on wider chalk and flint tracks, so to find a testing climb and steep singletrack descent linking back to the same starting point, as happens here south of Storrington, is a rare find. It is worth experimenting to see which of the two options you prefer as a climb or descent – they are interchangeable. Another wow factor on this ride is the steep descent into and climb out of the dry valley south of Amberley Mount – it is like entering a secret hidden kingdom. As ever, the best views of the day are from the wide track along the South Downs Way looking out over the patchwork countryside of the Weald below.

The Ride

Storrington has all you need for a starting point – pubs, cafés, a free car park and an exit on a flat quiet lane, giving you a bit of warm-up time before the daunting climb straight up the escarpment to the top of Kithurst Hill. Easy cruising leads to the hidden grassy kingdom mentioned above. The southern half of the ride is mainly through the Angmering Estate and has quite a different feel to the rest of the ride. The woods are a carpet of bluebells in the spring. Beyond the unexpectedly-located lawnmower centre at Myrtle Grove Farm, there is a long climb back up to the ridge, setting you up for a rooty, twisty descent back to Storrington.

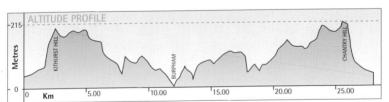

ALTITUDE PROFILE

Metres / 215 / 0

KITHURST HILL / BURPHAM / CHANTRY HILL

Km / 0 / 5.00 / 10.00 / 15.00 / 20.00 / 25.00

STORRINGTON & KITHURST HILL

GRADE: ▲

DISTANCE: 28KM

TOTAL ASCENT: 550M

START/FINISH: STORRINGTON, ON THE A283 NORTH OF WORTHING **GRID REFERENCE:** GR 088 144

PARKING: FREE CAR PARK BY TOURIST INFORMATION CENTRE AND LIBRARY OFF NORTH STREET IN STORRINGTON. GR 088 144

CAFÉ: LOTS OF CHOICE IN STORRINGTON. RIVERSIDE CAFÉ JUST OFF ROUTE IN AMBERLEY Tel: 01798 831 558

PUBLIC HOUSE: LOTS IN STORRINGTON. GEORGE & DRAGON, BURPHAM Tel: 01903 883 131. PUBS JUST OFF ROUTE IN AMBERLEY

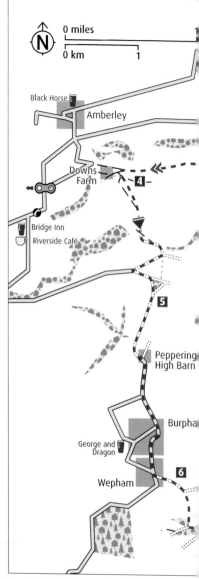

PULBOROUGH

P
S

A283

WASHINGTON

Storrington

Greyfriars Farm

2

South Downs Way

3

KITHURST HILL

13

12

11

Myrtle Grove Farm

10

Long Furlong Farm

A280

FINDON

Michelgrove

8 MAY BE MUDDY

9

Angmering Park

Storrington & Kithurst Hill

Directions – Storrington & Kithurst Hill

➊ From the Storrington Library car park, return to the main street (A283). Turn **R**, then **L** onto Church Street. Follow this past the church and onto a no through road. Continue in the same direction to the end of the tarmac.

2 At the fork by brown-brick Greyfriars Farm to the left, bear **R** on a wider track. The hill looms ahead. At a T-junction, turn **L** (blue arrow) then shortly, with a locked metal gate ahead, bear **R** very steeply uphill. Steep, then rideable, then steep again.

3 At the X-roads of tracks at the top, by a 4-way *Bridleway* signpost, go **SA**. At the X-roads with the South Downs Way, turn **R**. At the end of the wood, fork **R** to stay on the South Downs Way.

4 **Easy to miss**: after 2.5km, at the bottom of a steep grassy descent, with farm buildings in sight and about 100m after the end of the enclosed fenced section, turn **L** sharply back on yourself (red arrow). This wide chalk and earth track leads gently uphill. Shortly, bear **R** at a fork alongside the fence on the right, on a rough earth and grass track. Aim towards the bottom of the track that you can see climbing the hill ahead.

5 Steep descent. Climb on the obvious track ahead. Can you do it? At the T-junction with a broad stone track, by a 4-way signpost, turn **R**. Shortly, turn sharp **L** back on yourself, signposted *Bridleway*. Join tarmac at Peppering High Barn, then shortly, bear **L** at fork. At the next T-junction, bear **L*** ▶OR▷ steeply downhill.

* ▶OR▷ for the George and Dragon pub in Burpham, turn **R** then **R** again.

6 Climb, then 50m after passing a road to the right, take the next **L** on a broad concrete track, signposted *Bridleway*. This leads up past thatched Wepham Cottage. Climb steadily, then as the drive swings sharp left, bear **R** (in effect **SA**) downhill through a gate onto a chalk and stone track signposted *Bridleway*.

7 At the T-junction at the bottom of the hill, by an *Angmering Park Estate* signboard, turn **L**, then shortly, bear **R** uphill at the fork. Steep climb – how far can you go? At a 4-way *Bridleway* signpost, go **SA** (this can be muddy in winter). Shortly, by the next 5-way signpost, turn **L** on a tarmac road. **Ignore** turnings to right and left.

8   Continue **SA** as tarmac turns to track by a red-brick house. After 1.1km, at a T-junction, by a 3-way *Bridleway* signpost, turn **R**, signposted *Monarch's Way*. Shortly, at a 4-way signpost, turn **L** following *Monarch's Way* signs. The next section may be muddy, but there are alternatives on either or both verges.

9   After almost 1km, at another 4-way signpost, turn **L**, still following the Monarch's Way. Descend to exit the wood. Cross a field, then at the T-junction with the road, turn **L**. Shortly after passing a house called Michelgrove on the left and at the end of the wall on the right, turn **R** onto a broad stone track, signposted *Bridleway, Monarch's Way*.

10   Turn **R** through Myrtle Grove Farm, past a lawnmower centre, and join tarmac. At the T-junction with the road, turn **L** uphill towards Long Furlong Farm. Steady climb. Go through a bridlegate and the path becomes rougher alongside the fence to the left. Go through a second bridlegate into open pasture, with the fence now to the right.

11   Pass through a field gate at the bottom of a gentle descent. Start climbing gently, then after 200m, turn **R** through a bridlegate by a 3-way *Bridleway* sign. Short steep descent, then climb. **Easy to miss**: at the top of the climb, leave the wide chalk track and turn **L** uphill along the field edge, towards two small trees, signposted *Bridleway*.

12   At the T-junction with the South Downs Way, turn **L**. Go past the tall wooden signpost in the car parking area and follow the tarmac downhill. **Easy to miss**: keep your brakes on, then after 150m, turn sharp **L**, signposted *Bridleway*.

13   Climb gently, then after 600m, bear **R** at a fork by a 3-way *Bridleway* signpost, onto the lower grassy track curving away down the hillside. Keep bearing **L** down through the wood. Join tarmac by Greyfriars Farm and follow the outward route back to the start.

◄⊙◯ Making a day of it

Continuing 4km west on the South Downs Way links to the **Slindon** ride *(page 117)*. In the other direction, the South Downs Way over Sullington Hill joins the **Findon West** ride *(see page 129)* high above the A24.

18 Findon, Cissbury Ring & Sullington Hill

26km

Introduction

Findon is a fine little village, conveniently close to the A24 and Worthing. It offers many off-road options in the area enclosed by the coastal strip to the south and the A283 to the north and east. There are several pubs and other places for grabbing a bite. As Chanctonbury Ring is one of the most atmospheric spots on the whole course of the South Downs, it is visited on both of the rides starting from Findon. There is a tricky choice on this ride; do you go for a very bumpy descent leading to a safe (bridge) crossing of the A24 dual carriageway, or do you go for the excellent fast descent leading to a hairy crossing dodging the traffic? Both are signposted and described below.

The Ride

Thread your way down the narrow track, dropping down from Cissbury Ring to the A24. Climb, either off-road or on tarmac, depending how wet it has been, up to the ridge track that runs north up to Sullington Hill. A sharp right back along the South Downs Way leads to decision time about 'safe' or 'hairy' crossings of the A24. Grind that granny ring as you climb almost 150m up to the trees at the fantastic location of Chanctonbury Ring. A fine easy descent on broad tracks takes you back to Cissbury Ring.

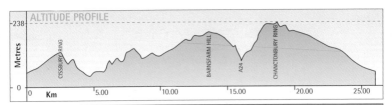

FINDON, CISSBURY RING & SULLINGTON HILL	GRADE: ▲
DISTANCE: 26KM	**TOTAL ASCENT:** 400M
START/FINISH: FINDON, JUST OFF THE A24 NORTH OF WORTHING	**GRID REFERENCE:** GR 121 089
PARKING: ON THE STREET CALLED 'THE SQUARE' IN FINDON	**CAFÉ:** VILLAGE HOUSE HOTEL, FINDON Tel: 01903 873 350
PUBLIC HOUSE: LOTS OF CHOICE IN FINDON. FRANKLAND ARMS, WASHINGTON Tel: 01903 892 220	

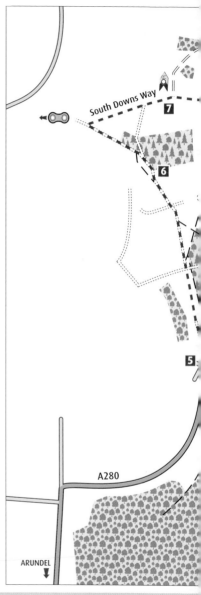

Frankland Arms
Washington

HORSHAM

Chanctonbury Ring

8

P

9

South Downs Way

A24

Gallops Farm

Village House Inn

10

Findon

S

P

2

A24

Cissbury Ring

MAY BE MUDDY

P

3

4

P

Worthing

0 miles 1

N

0 km 1

Findon, Cissbury Ring & Sullington Hill

Directions – Findon, Cissbury Ring & Sullington Hill

⊕ From the Village House Hotel in Findon, go **SA** onto The Square, following signs for *John Henry's Inn*. **Ignore** left and right turns until the end of the village. On a **RH** bend, turn **L** onto a no through road, signposted *Cissbury Ring* (white on blue sign).

2 Steady climb. At the end of tarmac, by a small car park to the left, turn **R** through a bridlegate by a *National Trust* sign. Head towards the *Cissbury Ring* signboard. Go through a second bridlegate to the **R** (blue arrow) towards the mast on the horizon. Stay close to the fence on the right, aiming for the copse.

3 Go through a metal gate onto a woodland track and fork **R** to descend more steeply (blue arrow). Narrow, possibly overgrown. Bear **R** to continue descending on this narrow track. At the X-roads with the A24, go **SA** onto a road called Bost Hill, signposted *6ft 9ins width limit*.

4 After 400m, at the end of trees, turn **R*** through a car park on a narrow, grassy bridleway, towards a small shed. The next section will be muddy after rain. At the end of the field on the left, at a X-roads of narrow bridleways, turn **L** uphill, at times steep. At the T-junction with a broader earth and stone track, bear **R**.

*To avoid mud after it has been raining, continue **SA** uphill on the road for a further 800m, then turn **R** onto West Hill, immediately before the windmill. Follow this road then track in the same direction for 3km and rejoin at *Instruction 5*.

5 At the X-roads with the busy A280, go **SA** onto the concrete track, signposted *Ashmarden Farm*. Continue **SA** on the track ahead, signposted *No vehicles*. At a X-roads of tracks, go **SA** onto a wide, grey gravel 'road'.

6 After about 1.5km, at a fork with a *Private Track* sign in the tree, bear **L** (GR 102 114). Shortly, at the next fork, bear **R** onto the narrower track that heads towards gates. At a new, open, wooden slat barn, turn **R** back on yourself. Follow the fence, now on your left, and join the South Downs Way as it heads east.

7 Decision time! After 1 km, you have the option of ▶ **(a)** turning **L** to use a bridge crossing of the A24 or ▶ **(b)** continuing **SA** downhill and crossing the fast dual carriageway. The descent towards the bridge crossing is much less fun, but you do avoid high-speed traffic.

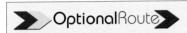

OptionalRoute

Option A:
Bridge crossing of the A24. Turn **L** off the main track, signposted *Alternative route avoiding A24*. Climb then descend on rough and bumpy track. At the bottom of the descent, bear **L** at a fork into the wood, signposted *South Downs Way*. Shortly join tarmac. As the road swings right after the first house, go **SA** on a short section of track, then **R** on a parallel road, following *South Downs Way* signs. At the T-junction at the bottom of The Street, turn **R**, signposted *South Downs Way*. After 1km, turn **L** on the first road sharply back uphill.

Option B:
Mixing with the traffic. Glorious descent to the A24. Take your time to plan your crossing of this fast road, allowing yourself time to gauge the speed of traffic. Cross following *South Downs Way* signs.

8 **Both routes.** Go through car park and climb. At a fork of tracks, shortly after a post with yellow and blue arrows, bear **L** uphill. At the T-junction at the top of a steep climb, turn **L**, signposted *South Downs Way* (red arrow).

9 About 500m after Chanctonbury Ring, at the summit, you will arrive at a X-roads of tracks, by a 4-way signpost. Turn **R**, signposted *Public Right of Way* (red arrow), leaving the South Downs Way.

10 After 2km, at a mega-junction of tracks, bear **R** (blue arrow). At the X-roads after the car park, turn **R** downhill, then **R** again at the bottom of the hill to return to Findon.

◄⊙⊙ Making a day of it

Another ride starts from **Findon**, exploring the tracks east towards the River Adur *(see page 135)*. To the west, a short section of the South Downs Way links you to the **Storrington** ride *(see page 123)*.

19 Findon, the Adur Valley & Chanctonbury Ring

26km

Introduction

Highlights of this ride include Cissbury Ring – you could easily do a circuit round the ring on bridleways. Then there's the ridge from Steep Down south east to Lancing, where the built-up area and the sea to the right contrast dramatically with the lovely valley and soft rolling fields to the left. But head and shoulders above them all is the ridge that leads to the atmospheric stand of trees on Chanctonbury Ring. This was massively damaged in the Great Gale of 1987 and will take a couple of generations before it fully regains its former glory.

The Ride

Climb east from Findon on tarmac to Cissbury Ring, then descend and climb again on track to the second highpoint on Steep Down. The peculiar shape of Lancing College, like a squat stone grasshopper, looms into view as you descend towards the River Adur. A long section on a quiet, flat lane in the valley gives you a chance to regain strength for an assault on the 235m climb, all the way up to Chanctonbury Ring. You deserve the descent that follows, which, with the exception of one short grassy climb north of Gallops Farm, leads all the way back to Findon.

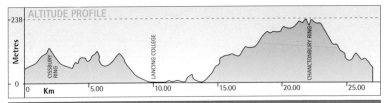

ALTITUDE PROFILE

Metres | 238 ... 0

CISSBURY RING | LANCING COLLEGE | CHANCTONBURY RING

Km | 0 | 5.00 | 10.00 | 15.00 | 20.00 | 25.00

FINDON, THE ADUR VALLEY & CHANCTONBURY RING   GRADE: ▲

DISTANCE: 26KM

START/FINISH: FINDON, JUST OFF THE A24 NORTH OF WORTHING

PARKING: ON THE STREET CALLED 'THE SQUARE' IN FINDON.

PUBLIC HOUSE: LOTS OF CHOICE IN FINDON. LOTS OF CHOICE JUST OFF THE ROUTE IN STEYNING

TOTAL ASCENT: 400M

GRID REFERENCE: GR 121 089

CAFÉ: VILLAGE HOUSE HOTEL, FINDON Tel: 01903 873 350

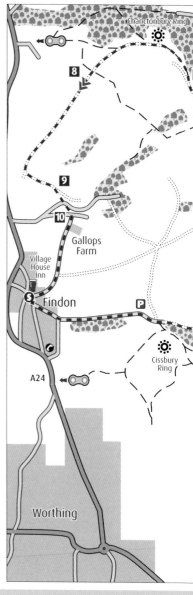

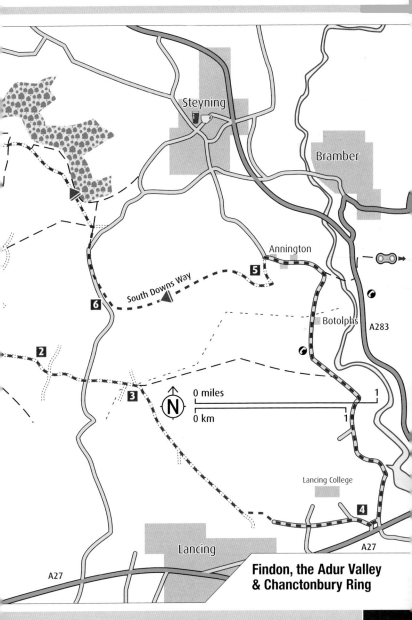

Steyning

Bramber

Annington

South Downs Way

5

6

Botolphs

A283

2

3

0 miles 1

0 km 1

N

Lancing College

4

Lancing

A27

A27

Findon, the Adur Valley & Chanctonbury Ring

Directions – Findon, the Adur Valley & Chanctonbury Ring

⊕ From the Village House Hotel in Findon, go **SA** onto The Square, following signs for *John Henry's Inn*. **Ignore** left and right turns until the end of the village. On a **RH** bend, turn **L** onto a no through road, signposted *Cissbury Ring* (white on blue sign). Steady climb. At the end of tarmac by a small car park to the left, continue **SA** downhill on a chalk track.

2 Superb downhill on mainly broad chalk and flint track. At the fork at the start of the climb take either track – they rejoin. At the X-roads of tracks at the top of the short steep climb, go **SA** to continue uphill towards the pylon on the horizon. At the X-roads with lane by a *Sompting* sign, go **SA** onto an undulating chalk and grass track, signposted *Bridleway*.

3 At the X-roads of tracks, pass to the **R** of the pylon, taking the track that climbs the hill between fences. Superb track with big views left, towards Adur Valley, and right, to built-up areas. Some mud in winter. Keep bearing **L**. Join tarmac by a *South Copse* sign. Lancing College comes into view. After 150m, on a sharp **RH** bend, bear **L** (in effect **SA**) onto a chalk and gravel track, signposted *Bridleway*.

4 At the T-junction with the Lancing College road at the bottom, bear **R**. At the road junction, just before the A27, with a house ahead, turn **L**. Shortly, turn **L** again, at a third T-junction, signposted *6ft 6ins width limit*.

5 Follow this lane for almost 5km, passing through Botolphs. Pass a cluster of houses in Annington and the drive to Annington House to the right. On a **RH** bend, turn **L** uphill on a broad earth and flint track, signposted *South Downs Way*. Steep climb, then gradient eases. Go through a gate into a huge field, with just a trace of a track. Vast grassy bowl to the right.

6 Long climb. Immediately before the road, turn **R** through a bridlegate on a track parallel to the road. Follow *South Downs Way* signs. Cross the road and continue climbing. At the X-roads of tracks by a flint memorial stone, go **SA** signposted *South Downs Way*.

7 Climb steadily. At the fork of tracks, bear **R**, following *South Downs Way* signs. At the X-roads of tracks by a 4-way signpost, continue **SA** uphill, signposted *South Downs Way* (red arrow).

8 Go past Chanctonbury Ring and continue **SA**, leaving the South Downs Way, which turns right. At several forks, take either track – they rejoin. At the T-junction with a similar wide chalk and stone track after a fast swooping descent, turn **L**.

9 Descend, climb, descend. At the top of the second climb, keep an eye out for a bridlegate to the **R**. Go through this onto a grassy track towards a second gate. At the X-roads with the lane, go through the bridlegate opposite and diagonally **L** uphill, across the pasture towards the next gate.

10 Exit the field and go **SA** uphill on a broad chalk and flint track. Go past Gallops Farm, joining a concrete track. Continue in the same direction on a tarmac lane. At the T-junction at the end of Stable Lane, turn **R** to return to start.

◄⦿⊃ Making a day of it

There is another ride that also starts from Findon, exploring the downland to the west of the A24 *(see page 129)*. In the other direction, a 10km section of the South Downs Way east from Annington *(Instruction 5, opposite)* leads past Truleigh masts and Devil's Dyke to the **Clayton Windmills** ride *(see page 141)* at Saddlescombe.

PHOTO BY NICK COTTON

20 Clayton Windmills & Wolstonbury Hill

20km

Introduction

There are three diversions off this ride that are worth contemplating; the first is to Jack & Jill Windmills, only a couple of hundred metres off the South Downs Way as you head west from Ditchling Beacon; the second diversion, the longest at about 2km, is a trip along the South Downs Way west from Saddlescombe Farm to gawp at Devil's Dyke – and maybe fit in a beer at the pub, the only option on the ride; the final diversion is to see the very fine Chattri war memorial, shaped like an Indian temple, as you climb up away from the built-up coast through the soft rolling green folds of the Sussex Downs on your way back up to the ridge.

The Ride

The ridge west of Ditchling Beacon is used on both the outward and return route. Follow this down close to the windmills and past the golf course to the busy A273. Is the bridleway parallel to this road the worst in Sussex for horse damage? Put it behind you as you climb up onto Wolstonbury Hill. Climbs and descents follow in quick succession as you cross two more ranges of hills. The most worthwhile of the three diversions mentioned left, to the extraordinary white Chattri temple and war memorial, is on the final long climb after the crossing of the A23, so you may well want a breather and a reality check that we have not been caught up in the slaughter of world wars.

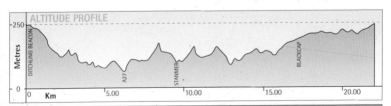

ALTITUDE PROFILE

250

Metres

0

DITCHLING BEACON

A27

STANMER

BLACKCAP

0   Km   5.00   10.00   15.00   20.00

CLAYTON WINDMILLS & WOLSTONBURY HILL   GRADE: ▲

DISTANCE: 20KM

START/FINISH: DITCHLING BEACON, NORTH OF BRIGHTON

PARKING: GR 332 131

PUBLIC HOUSE: DEVIL'S DYKE PUB (JUST OFF THE ROUTE) Tel: 01273 857 256

TOTAL ASCENT: 450M

GRID REFERENCE: GR 332 131

CAFÉ: BRING SANDWICHES

Clayton

Westmeston

BURGESS HILL

Jill

Jack

3

A273

2

New Barn Farm

Club House

HORSE ROOF MAGE

Ditchling Beacon

P

S

12

11

War Memorial

A23

10

9

A27

Brighton and Hove

Clayton Windmills & Wolstonbury Hill

Directions – Clayton Windmills & Wolstonbury Hill

➊ Follow the South Downs Way west from Ditchling Beacon car park. Shortly, at a fork of tracks, bear **R** on the lower track, signposted *South Downs Way*. Follow the obvious broad grassy track for 3.5km, with stunning views to the right.

2 **Easy to miss**: 200m before the windmills, turn sharp **L** on a wide smooth gravel track, signposted *South Downs Way*. At the X-roads of tracks about 100m after New Barn Farm, turn **R**, signposted *South Downs Way*. Go down past Pyecombe Golf Course.

3 At the busy A273, go **SA** signposted *South Downs Way* then turn **R**, signposted *Permissive bridleway*. This section is badly damaged by horses and will be muddy after rain. Climb steeply. At the T-junction with the lane turn **L**.

4 At the X-roads of tracks by a *National Trust Wolstonbury Hill* signboard, continue **SA** uphill through the bridlegate to the right, **not** through the field gate, which is locked. Climb to the brow and go through a bridlegate.

5 Descend through a second bridlegate. **Easy to miss**: after 250m, bear **L** at a fork of many paths on a track alongside the trees and scrub on the left. Go through a third bridlegate and turn sharp **L**. Roots and horse ruts. Join tarmac and cross the bridge over the A23.

6 Continue **SA** uphill on a narrow chalk track through two closely spaced bridlegates, then along a field edge. At a wooden post with two blue arrows, take the **LH** option on a narrow earth track that snakes its way up the hillside.

7 Go through a small clump of trees, through a bridlegate and follow the direction of the blue arrow, bearing **R** away from the line of gorse bushes to your left. Descend on an ever more obvious track. Immediately **before** a metal field gate, turn **L** through a bridlegate and **L** again steeply uphill.

8 After 150m, at the end of the woodland, turn **R** through a bridlegate onto a faint grassy track (GR 275 115). Pass through two more bridlegates, following blue arrows uphill to a metal bridlegate by a telegraph pole. Continue **SA** uphill beneath the power lines.

9   After 1.8km, at the barn (on the right) follow the track downhill to the **L**, signposted *Bridleway*. Join tarmac. **Easy to miss**: 30m after a sharp **RH** bend, turn **L** between concrete bollards then turn **R** before the railway bridge, following the tarmac track to cross the bridge over the A23.

10   At the T-junction turn **R**. Do not join the roundabout, but keep bearing **L**. At the brow of the hill, turn **L** on a lane and immediately bear **L** through a bridlegate, signposted *Downs on your doorstep no.40, Chattri & the Windmills*.

11   Aim for the telegraph pole carrying power lines, following a narrow grassy track across the field. Continue in the same direction, climbing gently through the next bridlegate towards a white monument* and a clump of trees on the horizon, ahead and to the right.

      *It is worth diverting 100m off the route to visit the Chattri War Memorial.

12   Long steady grassy climb. At the T-junction with the South Downs Way, turn **R** away from the windmills to rejoin the outward route and return to the start at Ditchling Beacon.

←🔗 Making a day of it

The **Ditchling Beacon & Stanmer Down** ride *(page 147)* shares the same starting point. If you follow the South Downs Way west for 10km from Saddlescombe, past Devil's Dyke and Truleigh masts, you will link to the **Findon East** ride *(page 135)* at Botolphs.

21 Ditchling Beacon & Stanmer Down

22km

Introduction

Ditchling Beacon is a bit of a mecca for mountain bikers, with the superb spine of the South Downs Way running east and west from one of the highest points along the whole trail. There are stunning views on a clear day and its proximity to Brighton and Hove means there is no shortage of people who can ride here from home. Indeed, for those seeking to persuade reluctant partners of the joys of mountain biking, you could do worse than take them for a spin along the ridge from Jack and Jill Windmills in the west to Blackcap in the east.

The Ride

You soon leave the South Downs Way as you head south on a grassy track that drops down into a secret valley, ending up at Lower Standean Farm. The track running close to the noisy A27 is one to put your head down and get out of the way as quickly as possible, but there are always the tearooms at Stanmer, with fine coffee and cakes to look forward to. The long steady climb up from near Falmer seems to go on forever, but it's all worth it as you emerge on the South Downs ridge for a very fine 4km blast along the top with the escarpment falling away steeply 150m down into the Sussex Weald.

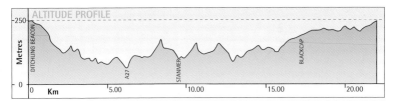

DITCHLING BEACON & STANMER DOWN	GRADE: ▲
DISTANCE: 22KM	**TOTAL ASCENT:** 330M
START/FINISH: DITCHLING BEACON CAR PARK, NORTH OF BRIGHTON	**GRID REFERENCE:** GR 332 131
PARKING: GR 332 131	**CAFÉ:** TEAROOMS IN STANMER Tel: 01273 604 041
PUBLIC HOUSE: THE SWAN, FALMER Tel: 01273 681 842	

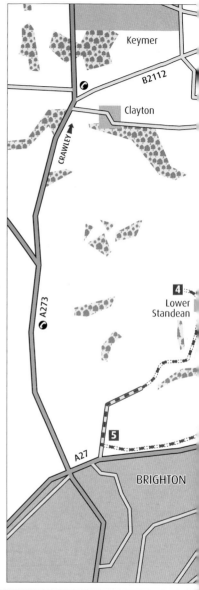

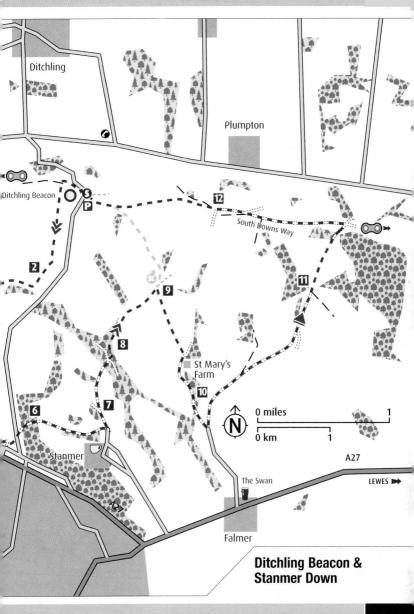

Ditchling

Plumpton

Ditchling Beacon

S
P

2

12

South Downs Way

9

11

8

St Mary's
Farm

10

7

6

0 miles   1

N

0 km   1

Stanmer

A27

The Swan

LEWES ➡

Falmer

Ditchling Beacon & Stanmer Down

Directions – Ditchling Beacon & Stanmer Down

➲ From the Ditchling Beacon car park, head west on the South Downs Way. **Easy to miss**: after 400m, immediately after a clump of trees and bushes to the left, you come to a wooden post with blue arrows. Turn **L** through a bridlegate, signposted *Heathy Brow*.

2 The rough track along a field edge improves and opens up in a big descent. At a fork by a 3-way signpost, bear **R** on smooth grass – no obvious track – down into the valley towards the woodland. Fantastic secret valley.

3 At the bottom of the descent, go **R** through a bridlegate (blue arrow) signposted *Downs on your doorstep no. 38*. Turn **L** to continue down the valley. Shortly, leave the valley floor and bear **R** uphill on a chalk and grass track at a fork by a signpost with a blue arrow and *No. 39*.

4 Climb steeply as the track swings **R** uphill through a gate, then descends to a bridlegate. Go through this and turn **L** on a broad gravel track past the farm.

5 Track turns to tarmac. After 2.5km, at tarmac T-junction, with the A27 just ahead, down below, turn **L**. The next section is noisy, close to the main road. Tarmac turns to stone track then grass and stone track. After 2km, just past a mini-roundabout on the right, follow the track as it turns **L** through a bridlegate. The track heads away from the road, uphill across pasture, on a narrow earth and stone surface and on towards woodland.

6 At the road, go **SA** onto a narrow track opposite. Continue in the same direction towards a metal barrier, signposted *Strictly no unauthorised vehicles beyond this point*. Tarmac descent.

7 After 1.5km at a T-junction with flint houses to the right, turn **L** uphill on track (or turn **R** for 200m for Stanmer Tearooms). Shortly, at a fork of broad gravel tracks, bear **R** along the **RH** field edge with the fence to your right. Continue climbing on a chalk track to the power lines.

8 At the brow of the hill by the pylon, continue **SA** downhill on a track signposted with a blue arrow *Number 6*. Lovely wooded descent. Go through a bridlegate, emerge from the woodland and continue along the **LH** field edge.

9 Follow the blue arrows as the track bears **R** out of the dry valley up to a bridlegate in the hedgerow. Go through this bridlegate and turn sharp **R*** OR on a rough grassy track keeping the hedge to your right.

* OR for short cut, turn **L** and climb for 2km back to Ditchling Beacon.

10 After 1km, go **SA** through St Mary's Farm on a concrete track. Climb, then 150m after the start of the descent (**easy to miss**) take the first narrow track **L*** OR through metal barriers, signposted *Bridleway*.

* OR continue **SA** for The Swan pub in Falmer.

11 Follow this track for 3km, passing beneath power lines and join a better chalk and flint track (the South Downs Way). At the T-junction by a 5-way sign, turn **L**, signposted *South Downs Way, Ditchling Beacon*.

12 After 2km, at a X-roads with a very narrow lane, continue **SA**. Views of Brighton. Follow for a further 1.5km back to the start at the X-roads with Ditchling Beacon.

← Making a day of it

This is the central one of three rides that all overlap. To the east is the **West of Lewes** ride *(page 153)* which links at Blackcap on the South Downs Way; to the west, also starting from Ditchling Beacon is the ride that explores Wolstonbury Hill *(page 141)*.

22 West of Lewes

35km

Introduction

This is one of the few rides graded black in the book, not because it is especially technical, but because it is long with a lot of climbing. The starting point of Kingston and the circuitous route at the beginning of the ride are there to avoid the traffic in Lewes and the busy road through Kingston. There are good quality tracks and fine views in all directions, with some fast descents and tough climbs to add to the mix. One of the most extraordinary descents in the book follows the old bullock track to the east of Woodingdean – a steady drop that seems to go on forever.

The Ride

The first time you do this ride you'll probably be scratching your head about the route from Kingston to the track running west from Lewes: there are lots of twists and turns to keep you well away from busy traffic. But once up onto the downs, everything falls into place: a fine stone then grass climb to Blackcap, a fast grassy blast downhill to cross the A27, then more of the same to the south of the main road, with a long climb to the masts and a long descent on the famous bullock track. The downs and ups continue until the final highpoint on Swanborough Hill, leaving you with a great downhill finish back to Kingston.

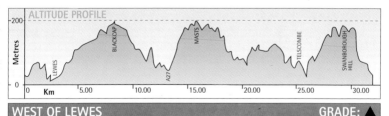

WEST OF LEWES	GRADE: ▲
DISTANCE: 35KM	**TOTAL ASCENT:** 700M
START/FINISH: JUGGS PUB IN KINGSTON NEAR LEWES	**GRID REFERENCE:** GR 393 082
PARKING: ON THE ROAD IN KINGSTON. GR 393 082	**CAFÉ:** LOTS OF CHOICE IN LEWES
PUBLIC HOUSE: THE JUGGS, KINGSTON Tel: 01273 472 523. MORE IN LEWES AND RODMELL	

Ovingdean

Woodingdean

Rottingdean

Saltdean

Telscombe Cliffs

Telscombe

BULLOCK HILL

MUDDY AFTER RAIN

South Downs Way

Rodmell

Iford

10
9
11
12
16
13
15
14

Directions – West of Lewes

6▸ Follow the no through road from Juggs pub in Kingston towards the church. Immediately after the church, turn **R** through a bridlegate onto a narrow tarmac path. At the end of the churchyard, turn **L** on the tarmac path. Go past tennis courts and emerge on Church Lane. Go **SA** as it starts to climb, then turns to track and narrows. At the T-junction with tarmac at a 3-way bridleway signpost, turn **R** downhill.

2 At X-roads go **SA** onto the lane opposite, signposted *Lewes, Ashcombe* (blue arrow). After 900m go through a bridlegate into a field on an obvious narrow earth track. Go through a second bridlegate into woodland (blue arrow). The track turns to tarmac.

3 Cross the A27 over a bridge. At the end of the grass of Jubilee Park to the left, turn sharp **L** by a flint wall, signposted *Bridleway*. Follow this narrow track, with fence and houses to the right. Ignore a left turn under a railway bridge. At the T-junction with a concrete track, with a railway bridge to the left and a new house ahead, turn **R**, signposted *Bridleway*.

4 Cross the busy road **SA** onto the lane signposted *Houndean Farm*. At a fork of tracks with a barn ahead bear **R** on the upper track. Shortly, at a post with a yellow arrow turn sharp **R** back on yourself uphill. Keep following blue arrows. At the end of the narrow field to the left turn **L** uphill then **L** again to follow the bridleway that now heads west.

5 Climb steadily for almost 2km on a narrow chalk and earth track through woodland, then on a grass track. Briefly join tarmac by farm and stables, continuing **SA** as tarmac turns back to track. Exit woodland out into the open with fine views. At a fork continue on the steeper track towards the **LH** edge of the woodland on the horizon.

6 Gentle descent. At a 5-way signpost by a bridlegate and a *National Trust Black Cap* information board, go through gate and turn **L**, signposted *South Downs Way, Housedean Farm*, A27. Surface trashed by horse hooves. **Easy to miss**: after 1km of gentle descent, keep an eye out for a wooden post with a blue arrow, directing the South Downs Way **L**, towards a pylon in the field to the left.

7 Great grass descent alongside the fence on the right, down through huge fields. With a stile and fence ahead, turn **R** through a bridlegate, signposted *South Downs Way*, to continue downhill. Descend, then climb very steeply through woodland. Second fast descent along a field edge.

8 At the T-junction with a tarmac path alongside the A27, turn **R**, signposted *South Downs Way, Southease via bridge over A27*. Bear **L** to follow path up and over the bridge. The road swings left. Just before rejoining the main road, continue **SA** through a bridlegate onto a narrow earth and stone track between hedge and fence, signposted *South Downs Way*. Follow the path **R** under the railway bridge, then **L**, signposted *South Downs Way*.

9 Climb steeply through woodland and several bridlegates, then more steadily for 2km along a field edge to the top and over the brow. At the T-junction with a wide stone track, turn **R** towards the masts.* **OR** Almost 1km past the masts and 50m **before** the road (by a double metal barrier), turn **L** sharply back on yourself, signposted *Bridleway to Rottingdean*.

   * **OR** turn **L** for a short cut to return to Kingston near Lewes.

10 **Easy to miss**: about 300m before a second mast, and just before the start of fencing that encloses a field this side of the mast, bear **L** onto a narrow grass track towards a bridlegate. Gentle descent over 3km, with stunning valley to the left. At the T-junction at the bottom, turn **R**.

11 **Easy to miss**: after almost 1km, at the end of an enormous field to the left and at the top of the first climb up from the valley floor, turn sharp **L** through a bridlegate and down a field edge (if you get to tarmac you have gone too far – retrace your steps 50m).

12 Descend, then climb steeply up the other side of this dry valley. At the brow, continue **SA** downhill past a red-brick ruin, then climb again. Shortly after a memorial cross to John Harvey, fork **R**. Continue in the same direction, following blue arrows for 2.6km on a long, gentle climb, then a short grassy descent.

DIRECTIONS CONTINUE ON NEXT PAGE

13 At a T-junction by a *Warning cattlegrids ahead* sign, turn **L**. This takes you through a bridlegate adjacent to a cattlegrid on a stone track that heads towards the white cliffs of Beachy Head. At the road turn **L**. Go through Telscombe, with its lovely white church. Climb. At the brow, bear **L** through a bridlegate onto a grass and stone track that runs parallel to and below the road (this will be muddy after rain).

14 After 1.5km, at the end of a run-down farm with lots of vehicle wrecks, at a 3-way wooden post, turn **L** signposted *South Downs Way*. This is a chalk and grass track that climbs steeply towards a house in the woods on the horizon. Go through a bridlegate and turn **L** on a narrow enclosed track to the right of the house (Mill Hill). Follow the South Downs Way down then up on a grass field-edge path. At the first concrete track, go **SA**.

15 At the second track junction, go **SA** on a wide concrete track, signposted *South Downs Way*, that climbs steadily. After 2.6km, as the track swings sharp left towards a barn, turn **R** at a 2-way wooden post, downhill, on a grassy track signposted *South Downs Way*.

16 **Ignore** turnings to the right and left for almost 2km, going **SA** at two wooden signposts. At a T-junction with a fence and a horse jump ahead, and a bridlegate to the left, turn **R** alongside the fence, at first flat on grass, then steeply downhill on chalk and stone. Tricky when wet.

17 At the start of tarmac and houses, turn **R** downhill by a 3-way signpost, between wooden bollards, on a gravel track. Join Church Lane, go past the tennis courts on a narrow tarmac path, then at the churchyard, at a X-roads of narrow tarmac paths, turn **R**. At the T-junction with the road turn **L** to return to the start.

◀━◉◯◯ **Making a day of it**

If you are looking for a real challenge, it is quite feasible to link this ride to the two rides that start from Ditchling Beacon for an 80km epic. Head west from Lewes and pick up the South Downs Way to Pyecombe (and Wolstonbury Hill) then return on the **Clayton Windmills** ride, the **Ditchling Beacon & Stanmer** ride and this, the **Lewes** ride, following each of them anti-clockwise. In the other direction, heading east, leave this ride shortly after Telscombe, and climb steeply on the South Downs Way to join the **Firle Beacon** ride.

23 Firle Beacon & a Taste of Toytown

16km

Introduction

Firle Beacon is the highpoint on the lump of land between two rivers that cut through the chalk of the South Downs; the River Ouse, south of Lewes, and the River Cuckmere, that passes through Alfriston. The Ram Inn at West Firle is a very fine pub with lots of tables outside. The nature of the ride means that it is one left for a day of good visibility, as the views out across the English Channel are stunning. Be prepared for a weird dislocation of your senses as you emerge from the rolling chalk downs and go through the newly built toytown on the edge of Seaford, before returning to the flint tracks.

The Ride

This ride starts and finishes with a downhill. Do the sums; that means that there is a big climb in the middle of it! Cruise down on easy tracks towards the coast, passing through the small hamlets of Norton and Bishopstone before the new neat estate houses on the edge of Seaford. Feel a bit out of place? Follow signs for the 'Bridleway to Bo Peep'(!) that leads across the golf course. Soon you are on the main climb of the ride, up onto Bostal Hill to join the South Downs Way and the highpoint at Firle Beacon. May the weather be with you.

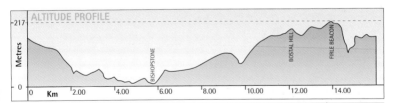

FIRLE BEACON & A TASTE OF TOYTOWN **GRADE:** ▲

DISTANCE: 16KM **TOTAL ASCENT:** 360M

START/FINISH: WEST FIRLE, SOUTH OF THE A27 BETWEEN EASTBOURNE AND LEWES **GRID REFERENCE:** GR 468 059

PARKING: FIRLE BEACON CAR PARK – TOP OF THE HILL SOUTH OF THE VILLAGE. GR 468 059 **CAFÉ:** BRING SANDWICHES

PUBLIC HOUSE: THE RAM INN, WEST FIRLE Tel: 01273 858 222

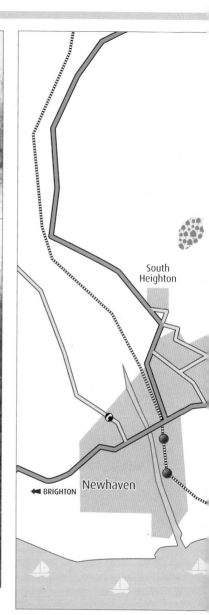

South
Heighton

◄ BRIGHTON   Newhaven

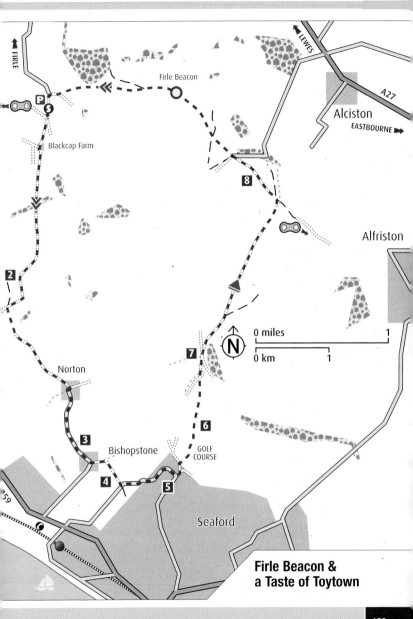

Firle

FIRLE

P
S

Blackcap Farm

Firle Beacon

LEWES

A27

Alciston

EASTBOURNE ▶

8

Alfriston

2

Norton

0 miles   1
N
0 km   1

7

3

Bishopstone

4   6

5   GOLF
             COURSE

Seaford

**Firle Beacon &
a Taste of Toytown**

Directions – Firle Beacon & a Taste of Toytown

➲ From the car park at the top of Firle Beacon, continue **SA** on tarmac, south towards the sea. After 700m, just before the final buildings of Blackcap Farm at the end of the tarmac lane, bear **L** (in effect **SA**). This takes you through a bridlegate, adjacent to a field gate, at the end of the flint wall and leads into a field. Keep the fence to the left.

2 Descend through several fields. Follow the grass track along the bottom of the dry valley. At a X-roads of grassy tracks, with a copse of trees 300m ahead, continue **SA** on a narrower track. The track swings **R** and climbs between hedgerows. At a junction of tracks at a 3-way signpost, turn **L** downhill.

3 Tarmac starts at the buildings. Go through the hamlet of Norton, bearing **R** at the fork, by a triangle of grass and a letterbox. Descend past *30mph* speed signs into Bishopstone. Short steep climb. At the brow, by a row of flint and brick cottages (Monksdean Barn), turn **L** uphill on a broad stone and gravel track, signposted *East Blatchington* (blue arrow).

4 Follow the blue arrows as the track bears **R** at two forks, climbing steeply to the brow, with a flint wall to the right and the sea ahead. At the T-junction with the road, turn **L**.

5 At the T-junction with Princess Drive at the end of Grand Avenue, turn **L**, then continue **SA** around metal barriers onto a tarmac path between wooden fences. At the next road (Royal Drive), turn **R**. At the T-junction, with Bowden House School ahead, turn **L** towards *No through road* signs. Shortly, and immediately before a *Seaford Golf Club* signboard, bear **L** around a metal field gate onto a concrete and grass track, signposted *Bridleway to Bo Peep*.

6 As the concrete track swings left, bear **R** through a bridlegate onto a faint, grassy track that leads towards the woodland ahead (blue arrow). Follow blue arrows as the route goes **SA** at several crossings with golf buggy trails and a concrete track.

7 At a junction of tracks, with a wooden bench dedicated to Paul Earl down to your left, cross the main track onto a narrow track between wooden gate posts, signposted *Access Land* (blue arrow). Fast descent, overgrown at the bottom. At a wooden signpost with two blue arrows, continue **SA** uphill on a wide, well-defined grass track.

8 Continue uphill, following the main track round to the **L***. The South Downs Way joins from the right. Go through a car park and a bridlegate, continuing **SA** uphill, following *South Downs Way* signs, to return to Firle Beacon.

*For a link to the *Alfriston* ride, at a lonesome 4-way signpost, turn **R** along the ridge, following the fence on the right. Go through a gate and at a X-roads, go **SA** onto a narrow woodland path, signposted *South Downs Way*. At the X-roads at the end of King's Ride, go **SA** onto Star Lane to arrive in the centre of Alfriston.

◄⊙⊙ Making a day of it

This ride can easily be linked to the **Alfriston** ride *(page 167)* by using the South Downs Way east of Bostal Hill *(Instruction 8)*. Similarly, if you can face a 190m climb up from the River Ouse, you can link via the South Downs Way west via Southease to the **Lewes** ride *(page 153)*.

PHOTO BY NICK COTTON

24 Alfriston, Friston Forest & Jevington

21km

Introduction

Alfriston is a tourist trap, with lots of pretty buildings, lots of people and loads of pubs, cafés and tea shops – try the bread pudding in the delicatessen in the square. Located on the Cuckmere River it means that rides start with a climb and finish with a descent. Alfriston to Eastbourne represents the last section of the South Downs Way, and the long distance trail certainly finishes with a bang rather than a whimper, with tough climbs and fantastic views out to sea. Friston Forest has a couple of waymarked rides. Apologies for not fitting in any woodland singletrack – it's impossible to describe, so get in there and explore for yourselves.

The Ride

Wiggle through the back streets of Alfriston to cross the footbridge over the Cuckmere and start climbing off-road. Each few metres, the views behind open up. From the top of Lullington Heath you dive down into Friston Forest on fast, open tracks. A mixture of climbs and descents on a variety of surfaces, brings you to the edge of woodland. From here, a steep then steady climb up over Willingdon Hill leads to the second highpoint and a smooth, fast grassy descent to Jevington. Chance for coffee or beer, then the final climb sets you up for one of the best open descents on the South Downs, from Windover Hill back down into Alfriston.

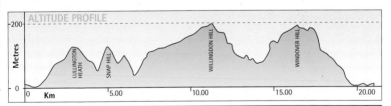

ALTITUDE PROFILE

ALFRISTON, FRISTON FOREST & JEVINGTON

GRADE: ▲

DISTANCE: 21KM

TOTAL ASCENT: 550M

START/FINISH: ALFRISTON, WEST OF EASTBOURNE

GRID REFERENCE: GR 518 035

PARKING: FROM THE SQUARE IN ALFRISTON, TAKE THE ROAD BETWEEN THE SMUGGLERS INN AND THE SINGING KETTLE TEASHOP. TURN SECOND LEFT ONTO NORTH ROAD & PARK NEAR THE SCHOOL. GR 518 035

CAFÉ: LOTS OF CHOICE IN ALFRISTON. JEVINGTON TEA GARDEN Tel: 01323 489 692

PUBLIC HOUSE: LOTS OF CHOICE IN ALFRISTON. EIGHT BELLS, JEVINGTON Tel: 01323 484 442

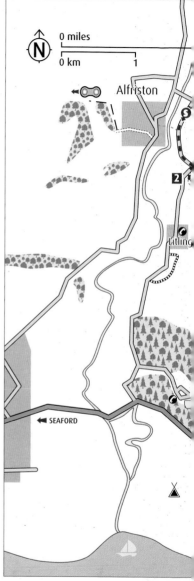

Directions – Alfriston, Friston Forest & Jevington

➲ From the market cross in the centre of Alfriston, take River Lane (no through road), opposite the Post Office. At the end, turn **R**, then after 150m, turn **L**, following *South Downs Way* signs, to cross the bridge over the river. Emerge on the road opposite Great Meadow Barn and turn **R**.

2 At the T-junction with Chapel Hill, turn **R**, signposted *Litlington*, then immediately after passing a wooden barn and a flint house to the right, turn **L** uphill on a broad stone track signposted *Jevington*.

3 Steady climb over 1.7km. At an obvious junction of tracks at the top of the climb, by a *Lullington Heath* signboard and a flint cairn, turn **R** alongside the fence.

4 After 1.4km, at the bottom of the fast, wide descent, go round a **LH** bend. This brings you to a mega-junction of tracks (GR 542 007). Turn **R** immediately before a metal field gate, uphill on a wide grass track signposted *Snap Hill*. Climb steeply and continue **SA** at 3-way signpost with blue arrows. At a X-roads with a major track by a 4-way post, go **SA**, signposted *Friston*.

5 Descend to a wide, smooth forest road and go **SA** uphill on a grass and stone track. Descend to cross a grassy gallop and re-enter woodland. At the next X-roads of tracks, continue **SA**, signposted *Friston* (blue arrow), soon running parallel to a tarmac lane to your right. Join this and continue in the same direction.

6 Cross the busy minor road **SA** through a bridlegate opposite, onto a grassy track that climbs steeply up through the field, signposted *Bridleway* (go straight up the hillside, not to the right as the signpost indicates). Continue in the same direction through a small patch of woodland and a second field towards and through a bridlegate. At the road, turn **L**.

7 Tarmac turns to stone, then stone and earth, then smooth grass, on a long, steady climb over almost 3km. Follow the track through a bridlegate next to a wide metal barrier, round to the **R**, to go past a clump of broadleaf trees. At a T-junction with a broad track, turn **L** to continue climbing gently. Go through two more bridlegates, then after 700m, at a major junction of tracks by a wooden post in a triangle of grass, continue **SA**, signposted *Butts Brow, Willingdon*.

8 Immediately before the barrier and car park, turn sharp **L** through a bridlegate, signposted *Bridleway to Jevington*. Superb, fast, smooth grassy descent. Continue through several bridlegates on a path along the field edge and through woodland. Head for the terraced houses in Jevington. At the T-junction at the end of Willingdon Lane, turn **R** then **L*** ▶OR▷ onto Church Lane, signposted *South Downs Way, Alfriston*.

* ▶OR▷ continue **SA** for 400m for the Eight Bells pub.

9 Climb steeply then more steadily. Go **SA** at a X-roads, signposted *South Downs Way* (blue arrow). Shortly, bear **L** at a T-junction to continue uphill. **Easy to miss**: at a X-roads of tracks in a small clearing near the end of woodland, at a 4-way signpost, turn **R**, signposted *South Downs Way* (blue arrow), onto a narrow, improved gravel track. Go through a bridlegate onto a smooth grass and stone field-edge path.

10 Climb gently on a smooth grass track, eventually following this 'roof of the world' path around the rim of a valley, down below to the left, keeping close to the fence on the left and aiming for the bridlegate on the horizon. Keep following the South Downs Way *'acorn'* symbol. Superb descent.

11 At the road, continue **SA** downhill on a good track. At the next road, turn **L** then **L** again, signposted *South Downs Way*. After 500m and shortly after a red triangular *Children* road sign, turn **R** opposite a flint building to the left, to rejoin the outward route. Cross the bridge over the river and follow the track to the **R**, signposted *South Downs Way for horses*, then round to the **L** to return to the centre of Alfriston.

◄●○ Making a day of it

There are a couple of waymarked trails in Friston Forest, one for families (green) and one a bit harder (purple). This ride could easily be linked to the **Firle Beacon** ride *(see page 161)* by following the South Downs Way west from the centre of Alfriston. Take Star Lane, opposite the George Inn, then follow King's Ride. Climb up onto Bostal Hill and join the **Firle Beacon** ride at *Instruction 8*. There are plenty more tracks to explore between Alfriston and Eastbourne.

top 10 Mountain bike playgrounds

There are several places along the North & South Downs that are either criss-crossed with bridleways and byways, or are owned by the Forestry Commission, with their relaxed, open access policy. These are suited to making up much shorter, personalised loops, taking in as much singletrack and technical bits as you can fit in.

For up-to-date information about other clubs and rides in the area go to the following websites: www.**kent-trails**.co.uk • www.**sussex-mtb**.com • www.**mountain-bike-guiding**.co.uk • www.**redlandstrails**.org

1 Puttenham Common, between Guildford and Farnham – Page 7
Lots of fine, well-drained sandy tracks, starting from main car park at GR 920 462. Also on Hankley Common and Ockley Common south of Elstead.   Maps: OS Landranger 186 or OS Explorer 145.

2 Woodlands between Guildford & Dorking – Pages 12, 21 & 29
Or more specifically the woods between Westhumble and Shere. Choose the time of year carefully as these vary enormously in stickiness from summer to winter.   Maps: OS Landranger 187 or OS Explorer 145 & 146.

3 Woodlands around Peaslake, south west of Dorking – Page 29
Includes the Summer Lightning trail at Leith Hill (see: www.redlandstrails.org/trails) and many tracks around Holmbury Hill and in Winterfold Wood.   Maps: OS Landranger 186 & 187 or OS Explorer 145 & 146.

4 King's Wood, south west of Canterbury – Page 65
Plus other Forestry Commission holdings around Canterbury, such as Clowes Wood to the north of the city, or Covert Wood, Elhampark Wood and West Wood to the south.   Maps: OS Landranger 179 or OS Explorer 137, 138 & 150.

5 Queen Elizabeth Country Park near Petersfield – Page 97
One easy and one moderate waymarked trail in the Forestry Commission woodland. A good base for Butser Hill and the South Downs Way.   Maps: OS Landranger 197 or OS Explorer 120.

South Downs escarpment south of Midhurst – Page 103

For downhill nuts. In the woodland, 5 miles east and west of the Cocking Hill car park (located on the A286, at GR 876 167).   Maps: OS Landranger 197 or OS Explorer 120 & 121.

South Downs escarpment west of Lewes – Page 141, 147 & 153

As above, there are a dozen testing descents from the ridge down the steep north slopes of the South Downs escarpment.   Maps: OS Landranger 198 or OS Explorer 122.

Friston Forest, west of Eastbourne – Page 167

One easy and one moderate waymarked trail in the woodland, plus access to the miles of bridleways stretching south east towards Beachy Head and north west to Alfriston and beyond.   Maps: OS Landranger 199 or OS Explorer 123.

Penshurst Off Road Club (PORC)

One of the few purpose-built mountain bike centres south of London, located near the small Kent village of Penshurst. See: www.porc-online.co.uk   Maps: OS Landranger 188 or OS Explorer 136.

Bedgebury Pinetum and woodland

Forestry Commission woodland east of Tunbridge Wells, where there are big plans to build new singletrack routes. There is also an easy off-road circuit of Bewl Water just to the west of the woods.
See: www.bedgeburypinetum.org.uk   Maps: OS Landranger 188 or OS Explorer 136.

top10 Climbs

*What is a good climb? One you can ride... just!
And if you don't ride it the first time, there's always
something to aim for next time around.*

Shalford, Albury & Abinger – Page 12

GR 097 481

Cross the level crossing north of Abinger, enter the broadleaf woodland and grind it out on chalk and flint tracks up onto the plateau (120m).

Shere & Polesden Lacey – Page 21

GR 073 480

Head north of Shere through thick broadleaf woodland on a track that can be a mudbath at the start, but gets better and better the higher you climb (120m).

Abinger & Leith Hill – Page 29

GR 142 432

Can you ride the final eastern approach up to Leith Hill Tower, highest point in South East England? All sorts of challenges – roots, steps and sand, this on top of the long steady climb you've already done south from Westcott to Coldharbour (total climb: 210m; the final challenge: 50m).

Reigate Hill, Stane Street & Box Hill – Page 35

GR 178 529

Long woodland lungbuster from Mickleham towards Box Hill. Popular with walkers so your pride won't let you walk! (150m).

Godstone & Oxted – Page 43

GR 375 434

Cross the roar of the M25 by Barrow Green Court and test your skills on this rooty, twisting number up onto Tandridge Hill (100m).

Butser Hill & East Meon – Page 91

GR **717 187**

The highest point on the South Downs, the climb up Butser Hill is WYSIWYG – what you see is what you get. The great grass slope rises up towards the mast and there is nowhere to hide (150m).

Goodwood & Hooksway – Page 103

GR **828 103**

Slippery when wet, the climb up onto Bow Hill and Kingley Vale Nature Reserve never lets up until you are right at the top, deep in the plantation of dark yew trees. (total climb: 160m; final challenge: 100m).

Storrington & Kithurst Hill – Page 123

GR **042 116**

Hidden in the folds of the South Downs, southeast of Amberley, is this jewel of a dry valley and the short, steep climb out of it will test to the limit your relationship with Granny Ring (70m).

Findon, Cissbury Ring and Sullington Hill – Page 129

GR **120 120**

The great grassy plateau around Chanctonbury Ring is a fine reward for the long pull up away from the A24 (130m).

West of Lewes – Page 153

GR **374 090**

There's a slight otherworldliness to the hills between the A27 and the sea, south of Lewes, as though they are stuck out on a limb. Or maybe it's just the lactic acid build up (155m).

top 10 Downhills

What's a good downhill? One that leaves you with a grin at the end. Here is a selection – obviously subjective and something to discuss endlessly over a beer.

1 **Shere & Polesden Lacey** – Page 21 GR 126 502
Never technical, the descent down towards Polesden Lacey does generate speeds where those washed out gullies across the path need some fast thinking about the line to take.

2 **Reigate Hill, Stane Street, Box Hill** – Page 35 GR 179 537
Drop down from Mickleham Downs to the Mole Valley through beautiful broadleaf woodland – always guaranteed to increase the sensation of speed.

3 **Wrotham & the North Downs Way** – Page 57 GR 598 601
Cross the bridge over the M20 and this is as close as it gets to technical in the North Downs. Very tricky when wet.

4 **Butser Hill & East Meon** – Page 91 GR 712 201
It's a WYSIWYG climb (see Uphills) and it's a WYSIWYG downhill!

5 **Goodwood & Hooksway** – Page 103 GR 849 172
Ah, if only all rides could finish like this; 140m of descent charging down a hillside at the end of a long cruising section with great views.

Slindon & Bignor Hill – Page 117

GR 951 102

This must be just the right gradient to let it rip and just the right curves to give you that gliding/dancing sensation.

Storrington & Kithurst Hill – Page 123

GR 085 125

About as technical as it gets in the South Downs. Twisty, rooty, steep singletrack. Why not try as a downhill the climb up from Storrington used on this ride?

Findon, Cissbury Ring and Sullington Hill – Page 129

GR 105 120

There are two ways to descend to the A24 – one takes you down to a safe footbridge and is a bit of a disappointment. By contrast this option is a belter and even more exciting when wet. But it leaves you dodging fast traffic to cross the dual carriageway. Decisions, decisions!

West of Lewes – Page 153

GR 365 065

This extraordinary track from Bullock Hill down towards Rottingdean was built for beasts of burden and the downhill gradient is like balm to the soul.

Alfriston, Friston Forest & Jevington – Page 167

GR 546 032

One minute you are on a grassy roof-of the-world plateau and the next you're on a white-knuckle rollercoaster of a descent, dropping 190m down to the honeypot of Alfriston. Grin, baby, grin.

Appendices

Bike Shops

There are many bike shops on or close to the rides in this book, from the ubiquitous Halfords, several well known cycle chains (ha ha) right down to the small dedicated local dealer. Listed below is a selection of shops which we have found to be particularly helpful to the local mountain biker.

Cycles UK
147–148 Milton Road
Gravesend
T: 01474 333 090   www.**cyclesuk**.com

Cycles UK
21–25 Lower Stone Street
Maidstone
T: 01622 688 162   www.**cyclesuk**.com

East Street Cycles
Unit 6
The Woolmead
Farnham
T: 01252 723 888   www.**eaststcycles**.com

Evans Cycles
4 Air Street
Brighton
T: 0845 070 5407

Evolution Cycles
23a Cavendish Place
Eastbourne
T: 01323 737 320   www.**evocycles**.co.uk

Finch & Son
43 Bell Street
Reigate
T: 01737 242 163   www.**finchcycles**.co.uk

Godalming Cycles
2 Angel Court
Godalming
T: 01483 420 036 www.**godalmingcycles**.co.uk

Head For The Hills
43 West Street
Dorking
T: 01306 885 007 www.**head-for-the-hills**.co.uk

Mr Cycles
26 Clinton Place
Seaford
T: 01323 893 130   www.**mrcycles**.co.uk

Owens Cycles
Stoner Hill
Steep
Petersfield
T: 01730 260 446   www.**owenscycles**.co.uk

Peter Hansford Cycles
91 Olivers Battery Road South
Winchester
T: 01962 877 555   www.**peterhandsford**.co.uk

Quest Adventure
5 Ardsheal Road
Broadwater
Worthing
T: 01903 573 700   www.**questadventure**.co.uk

South Downs Bikes Ltd.
The Forge
38 West Street
Storrington
T: 01903 745 208 www.**southdownsbikes**.com

Tibbs Cycle Store
22 Stour Street
Canterbury
T: 01227 787 880   www.**tibbscyclestore**.co.uk

Trev's Cycles Centre
3a High Street
Ashford
T: 01233 641 310

Tri the Bike Shop
18 Windmill Street
Gravesend
T: 01474 533 748   www.**trithebike**.co.uk

Tourist Information Centres

Arundel	T: 01903 882 268
Ashford	T: 01233 629 165
Brighton	T: 0906 711 2255
Canterbury	T: 01227 378 100
Chichester	T: 01243 775 888
Eastbourne	T: 0906 711 2212
Faversham	T: 01795 534 542
Guildford	T: 01483 444 333
Lewes	T: 01273 483 448
Maidstone	T: 01622 602 048
Midhurst	T: 01730 817 322
Petersfield	T: 01730 268 829
Petworth	T: 01798 343 523
Seaford	T: 01323 897 426
Sevenoaks	T: 01732 450 305
Winchester	T: 01962 840 500
Worthing	T: 01903 221 066

Weather

www.bbc.co.uk/weather OR www.metoffice.com

Food and Drink

One of the joys of mountain biking in an area as populated as the South East, is that you are never far away from a good pub or café. There are far too many pubs to mention, but The Good Pub Guide always helps if you want to plan your route around the pubs – and there are a few good websites:

www.beerintheevening.com
www.pubutopia.com
www.pubsgalore.co.uk

I know of no similar websites listing cafés and tea rooms, but here are a few recommendations:

The Barn Café T: 01483 222 820
Newlands Corner, near Guildford.

Reigate Hill car park café (outdoors).

Queen Elizabeth Country Park Visitor Centre
T: 023 9259 5040, Petersfield.

The Hiker's Café (outdoors), at the junction of the A29 and A284 north of Arundel.

Stanmer Tearooms T: 01273 604 041
North east of Brighton.

Jevington Tea gardens T: 01323 489 692
West of Eastbourne.

Accommodation

For youth hostels visit **www.yha.org.uk**. There are hostels in the following places on or near the routes described:

Alfriston	T: 0870 770 5666
Arundel	T: 0870 770 5676
Brighton	T: 0870 770 5724
Canterbury	T: 0870 770 5744
Holmbury St Mary (Dorking)	T: 0870 770 5868
Tanners Hatch (Dorking)	T: 0870 770 6060
Telscombe (Lewes)	T: 0870 770 6062

Hotels, Self-Catering and B&B

Try the internet or the nearest Tourist Information Centre. Expect to pay more than in other parts of the country.

Camping

Try the following websites:
www.enjoyengland.com
www.camping.uk-directory.com
www.find-a-campsite.co.uk
www.ukcampsite.co.uk

The Author

Nick Cotton has written over 30 bike guides in the last 12 years, riding more than 20,000 miles all over Britain during the course of his research. He has travelled and trekked extensively, climbing to over 18,000ft on three continents and has cycled in Morocco and Patagonia (the worst winds in the world!).

He lives in the Lune Valley in Cumbria, between the Lakes and the Dales. He is very partial to fine coffee, real ale and cakes, especially on the course of a ride. Six feet four and 14 stones needs a lot of fuel.

The Photographer

At the end of each Peak District ride, Andy regrets living at the top of a big, steep hill on the outskirts of Matlock. A professional sports photographer, his twenty years as a mountain biker have included trips to Ethiopia, Romania, Morocco and China, and racing wins in *Polaris*, *Trailquest* and the 1,097-mile *Iditasport Impossible* across Alaska. He can be contacted on **01629 580 780** or at **andrew.heading@btopenworld.com**

Vertebrate Graphics

Vertebrate Graphics (VG) is Britain's leading graphic design agency that specialises in the outdoor leisure market. Based deliberately near the Peak District, the guidebook production team spend as much time as they can walking, riding and climbing in the Peak District. We have had substantial success in the design and production of specialist outdoor books. These include *Hillwalking – The Official Handbook of the Mountain Leader and Walking Group Leader Schemes* (a bestselling outdoor title for three years running), highly praised rock climbing guidebooks such as *The Roaches – Staffordshire Grit* and the UK's best selling mountain bike guide: *Dark Peak Mountain Biking – True Grit Trails*.

VG produce printed literature, advertising and websites, for more details of our services please refer to our website at: **www.v-graphics.co.uk** or email us at: **info@v-graphics.co.uk**

Order form for
Vertebrate Publishing
Publications

Fill in this coupon and send
it along with a cheque to:
Vertebrate Graphics
Crescent House
228 Psalter Lane
Sheffield S11 8UT

Please make cheques payable
to **Vertebrate Graphics Ltd**.
Credit card payments are
accepted on our website.
Orders dispatched by return.

Item	Qty	Price (inc.P&P)
Dark Peak MTB Guide Book		£14.95
Dark Peak CD-ROM		£7.50
Dark Peak Bundle (Book & CD-ROM)		£20.00
White Peak MTB Guide Book		£14.95
White Peak CD-ROM		£7.50
White Peak Bundle (Book & CD-ROM)		£20.00
South West MTB Guide Book		£14.95
South West CD-ROM		£7.50
South West Bundle (Book & CD-ROM)		£20.00
Lake District MTB Guide Book		£15.95
Lake District CD-ROM		£7.50
Lake District Bundle (Book & CD-ROM)		£21.00
Yorkshire Dales North MTB Guide Book		£15.95
Yorkshire Dales North CD-ROM		£7.50
Yorkshire Dales North Bundle (Book & CD-ROM)		£21.00
Yorkshire Dales South MTB Guide Book		£15.95
Yorkshire Dales South CD-ROM		£7.50
Yorkshire Dales South Bundle (Book & CD-ROM)		£21.00
South East N&S Downs MTB Guide Book		£15.95
South East N&S Downs CD-ROM		£7.50
South East N&S Downs Bundle (Book & CD-ROM)		£21.00
Cycling in the Peak District MTB Guide Book		£12.95
Off-road Trails & Quiet Lanes MTB Guide Book		£12.95
	TOTAL £	

Name: ....

Address: ....

....

Postcode: ....

E-mail: ....

Vertebrate Graphics will never pass on your details to third parties, but if you do not want to receive information on future
VG Hill Walking, Mountain Biking or Climbing and Bouldering Guides, please tick here ☐

MountainBiking RouteCDs

All the maps, descriptions, **bonus routes** and **extras**, in print-ready files for your PC or Mac.

Save weight! Leave the books behind and just pack the maps and descriptions you need.

Only £7.50
each including postage & packing

The CDs are MAC and PC compatible, and need Adobe® Reader® to run (Adobe® Reader® is available free of charge from www.adobe.com)

You can use the order form on the reverse of this page or order directly from the publications section of our website.

For orders and more information check out:
www.v-outdoor.co.uk